Contents

Preface

The NHS is the public service most valued by the British people. Ever since its creation in 1948, the NHS has been available when we've needed it and has removed the fear of paying for treatment when we are ill. Its founding principles of providing access to care to all on the basis of need, not ability to pay, remain as important today as in 1948. In an age when our lives and jobs are undergoing constant change, it is reassuring to know that the NHS is there and will take care of us in times of need.

Yet despite its many achievements, the NHS has failed to keep pace with changes in our society. Too often patients have to wait too long. There are unacceptable variations in standards across the country. What patients receive depends too much on where they live and the NHS has yet to fulfil the aspiration to provide a truly national service. Constraints on funding mean that staff often work under great pressure and lack the time and resources they need to offer the best possible service.

To tackle these problems, the government has decided to make an historic commitment to increase the funding of the NHS over the next four years. The Prime Minister's announcement in March of large, sustained investment in the NHS provides the funding that doctors, nurses, dentists, therapists, managers and other staff have called for over the years.

More money is, however, only the starting point. The challenge is to use the resources available to achieve real benefits for patients and to ensure that the NHS is modernised to meet modern public expectations. That is why in announcing the increase in funding for the NHS the Prime Minister set five challenges that needed to be addressed: partnership; performance; professions and the wider NHS workforce; patient care; and prevention.

Since March, NHS staff, patients' representatives and others have responded to these challenges through the work undertaken by the Modernisation Action Teams. The teams have undertaken a detailed analysis of the problems facing the NHS in their area, informed by the results of public and staff consultation. There has also been consultation with NHS frontline staff, with patients and the public and with representative groups. It is this inclusive process that has shaped the contents of this NHS Plan. Implementing the policies set out in the Plan also calls for an inclusive approach, to ensure that the resources now available really do produce a step change in results.

While each of us may have different views on individual components of the Plan, we all support the process of modernisation and reform, and welcome the direction of travel: to reshape the NHS from a patient's point of view.

Underpinning the Plan are a set of core principles. The importance of these principles is that they represent the common ground between the Government and the NHS as the task of modernising and rebuilding the health service begins. Some of the principles restate the founding values of the NHS, others reflect issues that are important today. Taken together they offer a framework for taking forward the programme set out in this Plan.

NHS core principles

We the undersigned support these principles, and commit ourselves to a modernised NHS on the basis of these principles reflected in this NHS Plan.

1. The NHS will provide a universal service for all based on clinical need, not ability to pay.

Healthcare is a basic human right. Unlike private systems the NHS will not exclude people because of their health status or ability to pay. Access to the NHS will continue to depend upon clinical need, not ability to pay.

2. The NHS will provide a comprehensive range of services

The NHS will provide access to a comprehensive range of services throughout primary and community healthcare, intermediate care and hospital based care. The NHS will also provide information services and support to individuals in relation to health promotion, disease prevention, self-care, rehabilitation and after care. The NHS will continue to provide clinically appropriate cost-effective services.

3. The NHS will shape its services around the needs and preferences of individual patients, their families and their carers

The NHS of the 21st century must be responsive to the needs of different groups and individuals within society, and challenge discrimination on the grounds of age, gender, ethnicity, religion, disability and sexuality. The NHS will treat patients as individuals, with respect for their dignity. Patients and citizens will have a greater say in the NHS, and the provision of services will be centred on patients' needs.

4. The NHS will respond to different needs of different populations

Health services will continue to be funded nationally, and available to all citizens of the UK. Within this framework, the NHS must also be responsive to the different needs of different populations in the devolved nations and throughout the regions and localities. Efforts will continually be made to reduce unjustified variations and raise standards to achieve a truly National Health Service.

5. The NHS will work continuously to improve quality services and to minimise errors

The NHS will ensure that services are driven by a cycle of continuous quality improvement. Quality will not just be restricted to the clinical aspects of care, but include quality of life and the entire patient experience. Healthcare organisations and professions will establish ways to identify procedures that should be modified or abandoned and new practices that will lead to improved patient care. All those providing care will work to make it ever safer, and support a culture where we can learn from and effectively reduce mistakes. The NHS will continuously improve its efficiency, productivity and performance.

6. The NHS will support and value its staff

The strength of the NHS lies in its staff, whose skills, expertise and dedication underpin all that it does. They have the right to be treated with respect and dignity. The NHS will continue to support, recognise, reward and invest in individuals and organisations, providing opportunities for individual staff to progress in their careers and encouraging education, training and personal development. Professionals and organisations will have opportunities and responsibilities to exercise their judgement within the context of nationally agreed policies and standards.

7. Public funds for healthcare will be devoted solely to NHS patients.

The NHS is funded out of public expenditure, primarily by taxation. This is a fair and efficient means for raising funds for healthcare services. Individuals will remain free to spend their own money as they see fit, but public funds will be devoted solely to NHS patients, and not be used to subsidise individuals' privately funded healthcare.

8. The NHS will work together with others to ensure a seamless service for patients.

The health and social care system must be shaped around the needs of the patient, not the other way round. The NHS will develop partnerships and co-operation at all levels of care – between patients, their carers and families and NHS staff; between the health and social care sector; between different Government departments; between the public sector, voluntary organisations and private providers in the provision of NHS services – to ensure a patient-centred service.

9. The NHS will help keep people healthy and work to reduce health inequalities

The NHS will focus efforts on preventing, as well as treating ill-health. Recognising that good health also depends upon social, environmental and economic factors such as deprivation, housing, education and nutrition, the NHS will work with other public services to intervene not just after but before ill health occurs. It will work with others to reduce health inequalities.

10. The NHS will respect the confidentiality of individual patients and provide open access to information about services, treatment and performance

Patient confidentiality will be respected throughout the process of care. The NHS will be open with information about health and healthcare services. It will continue to use information to improve the quality of services for all and to generate new knowledge about future medical benefits. Developments in science such as the new genetics offer important possibilities for disease prevention and treatment in the future. As a national service, the NHS is well-placed to take advantage of the opportunities offered by scientific developments, and will ensure that new technologies are harnessed and developed in the interests of society as a whole and available to all on the basis of need.

Now the challenge is to translate the Plan into practice and to show over a period of years that the NHS really can be modernised. We believe this is possible because the NHS is already providing, in some places, the kind of service which needs to be available to all patients in the future. The task now, as Nye Bevan said at the inception of the NHS, is to 'universalise the best' as we implement the principles that underpin the Plan.

We look forward to working with the Government in modernising the NHS and ensuring change is delivered across health and social care. All of us have a critical role in making this happen.

Prof Sir George Alberti *President*
Royal College of Physicians of London

Christine Hancock *General Secretary*
Royal College of Nursing

Barry Jackson *President*
Royal College of Surgeons of England

Bob Abberley *Head of Health*
UNISON

Prof Mike Pringle *President*
Royal College of General Practitioners

Karlene Davis *General Secretary*
Royal College of Midwives

Dr Ian Bogle *Chairman of Council*
British Medical Association

Dr Jenny Simpson *Chief Executive*
British Association of Medical Managers

Stephen Thornton *Chief Executive*
NHS Confederation

Sir Jeremy Beecham *Chair*
Local Government Association

Dr Michael Dixon *Chairman*
NHS Alliance

Harry Cayton *Chief Executive*
Alzheimer's Society

P. Smith

Dr Peter Smith *Chair*
National Association of Primary Care

Julia N...

Rabbi Julia Neuberger *Chief Executive*
Kings Fund

James McEwen

Prof James McEwen *President*
Faculty of Public Health Medicine

Natalie Beswetherick

Natalie Beswetherick *Chair*
Allied Health Professions Forum

Melinda Letts

Melinda Letts *Chairwoman*
Long Term Medical Conditions Alliance

Barbara Meredith

Barbara Meredith *Policy and Communications Manager* Age Concern London and The Patients Forum

Delyth Morgan

Delyth Morgan *Chief Executive*
Breakthrough Breast Cancer

Diana Whitworth

Diana Whitworth *Chief Executive*
Carers National Association

Eoin M. Redahan

Eoin Redahan *Director of Public Relations* The Stroke Association

Bob Gann

Bob Gann *Director*
The Help for Health Trust

Paul R. Streets

Paul Richard Streets *Chief Executive*
Diabetes UK

Alexander Macara

Sir Alexander Macara *Chairman*
National Heart Forum

Nicholas Young

Sir Nicholas Young *Chief Executive*
Macmillan Cancer Relief

Foreword by the Prime Minister

For people of my father's generation, the creation of the NHS in 1948 was a seminal event. No longer would wealth determine access to healthcare; need, irrespective of ability to pay, would be the criterion. To a generation brought up with the jar on the mantlepiece for the doctor's fee and dread if a child fell ill, the NHS was an extraordinary act of emancipation.

For that reason, the NHS retains, in its essential values, huge public support. But over twenty years, it has struggled. Its funding has not kept pace with the healthcare systems of comparable countries. Its systems of working are often little changed from the time it was founded, when in the meantime virtually every other service we can think of has changed fundamentally.

So urgent was the need for extra money for the NHS that many of the failures of the system were masked or considered secondary. In March we took a profound decision as a Government. We had sorted out public finances. Debt repayments were down. Spending on unemployment benefits and other benefits associated with large numbers of people economically inactive, was down also. We decided to make an historic commitment to a sustained increase in NHS spending. Over five years it amounts to an increase of a third in real terms. Over time, we aim to bring it up to the EU average.

In doing so, we offered the nation and those in the NHS a deal. We would spend this money if, but only if, we also changed the chronic system failures of the NHS. Money had to be accompanied by modernisation; investment, by reform. For the first time in decades we had to stop debating resources; and start debating how we used them to best effect.

Over the past few months the NHS and its staff have risen magnificently to this challenge. Many have been working flat out in a system they never had the chance to question. There have been teams of NHS professionals and others analysing each part of our healthcare system and how it can be improved. Personally, I have been having four or five meetings each week, as well as seeing scores of people from every part of the NHS.

Together we have produced this Plan for the future of the NHS. At every level there will be radical change. It will, of course, take time to achieve it all. But, taken as a whole, it does offer the genuine opportunity to re-build the NHS for the 21st century, true to its priorities but radically reformed in their implementation. It is, in a very real sense, our chance to prove for my generation and that of my children, that a universal public service can deliver what the people expect in today's world. For all of us it is a challenge. But it is one we intend to meet.

Tony Blair

Executive summary

This is a Plan for investment in the NHS with sustained increases in funding. This is a Plan for reform with far reaching changes across the NHS. The purpose and vision of this NHS Plan is to give the people of Britain a health service fit for the 21st century: a health service designed around the patient. The NHS has delivered major improvements in health but it falls short of the standards patients expect and staff want to provide. Public consultation for the Plan showed that the public wanted to see:

- more and better paid staff using new ways of working

- reduced waiting times and high quality care centred on patients

- improvements in local hospitals and surgeries,

In part the NHS is failing to deliver because over the years it has been underfunded. In particular there have been too few doctors and nurses and other key staff to carry out all the treatments required. But there have been other underlying problems as well. The NHS is a 1940s system operating in a 21st century world. It has:

- a lack of national standards

- old-fashioned demarcations between staff and barriers between services

- a lack of clear incentives and levers to improve performance

- over-centralisation and disempowered patients.

These systematic problems, which date from 1948 when the NHS was formed, are tackled by this Plan. It has examined other forms of funding healthcare – and found them wanting. The systems used by other countries do not provide a route to better healthcare. The principles of the NHS are sound but its practices need to change.

The March 2000 Budget settlement means that the NHS will grow by one half in cash terms and by one third in real terms in just five years. This will fund extra investment in NHS facilities…

- 7,000 extra beds in hospitals and intermediate care

- over 100 new hospitals by 2010 and 500 new one-stop primary care centres

- over 3,000 GP premises modernised and 250 new scanners

- clean wards – overseen by 'modern matrons' – and better hospital food

- modern IT systems in every hospital and GP surgery

…and investment in staff:

- 7,500 more consultants and 2,000 more GPs

- 20,000 extra nurses and 6,500 extra therapists

- 1,000 more medical school places

- childcare support for NHS staff with 100 on-site nurseries.

But investment has to be accompanied by reform. The NHS has to be redesigned around the needs of the patient. Local hospitals cannot be run from Whitehall. There will be a new relationship between the Department of Health and the NHS to enshrine the trust that patients have in frontline staff. The principles of subsidiarity will apply. A new system of earned autonomy will devolve power from the centre to the local health service as modernisation takes hold.

The Department of Health will set national standards, matched by regular inspection of all local health bodies by the Commission for Health Improvement. A more streamlined centre will merge the posts of Permanent Secretary and Chief Executive creating one post which will be appointed in the autumn.

The National Institute for Clinical Excellence will ensure that cost effective drugs like those for cancer are not dependent on where you live. A Modernisation Agency will be set up to spread best practice.

Local NHS organisations that perform well for patients will get more freedom to run their own affairs. There will also be a £500 million performance fund. But the Government will intervene more rapidly in those parts of the NHS that fail their patients.

For the first time social services and the NHS will come together with new agreements to pool resources. There will be new Care Trusts to commision health and social care in a single organisation. This will help prevent patients – particularly old people – falling in the cracks between the two services or being left in hospital when they could be safely in their own home.

For the first time there will be modern contracts for both GPs and hospital doctors. NHS doctors work hard for the NHS. But the contracts under which they work are outdated. There will be a big extension of quality-based contracts for GPs in general, and for single-handed practices in particular. The number of consultants entitled to additional discretionary payments will rise from half to two-thirds but in return they will be expected to increase their productivity while working for the NHS. Newly qualified consultants will not be able to do private work for perhaps seven years.

For the first time nurses and other staff not just in some places, but everywhere will have greater opportunity to extend their roles. By 2004 over half of them will be able to prescribe medicines. £280 million is being set aside over the next three years to develop the skills of staff. All support staff will have an Individual Learning Account worth £150 per year. The number of nurse consultants will increase to 1,000 and a new role of consultant therapist will be introduced. A new Leadership Centre will be set up to develop a new generation of managerial and clinical leaders, including modern matrons with authority to get the basics right on the ward.

For the first time patients will have a real say in the NHS. They will have new powers and more influence over the way the NHS works:

• letters about an individual patient's care will be copied to the patient

• better information will help patients choose a GP

• patient advocates and advisers will be set up in every hospital

• proper redress when operations are cancelled on the day they are due to take place

• patients' surveys and forums to help services become more patient-centred.

For the first time there will be a concordat with private providers of healthcare to enable the NHS to make better use of facilities in private hospitals – where this provides value for money and maintains standards of patient care. NHS care will remain free at the point of delivery – whoever provides it.

These far reaching reforms to the service will result in direct improvements for patients.

Patients will see waiting times for treatment cut as extra staff are recruited:

• by 2004 patients will be able to have a GP appointment within 48 hours and there will be up to 1,000 specialist GPs taking referrals from fellow GPs

- long waits in accident and emergency departments will be ended

- by the end of 2005 the maximum waiting time for an outpatient appointment will be three months and for inpatients, six months.

The treatment of cancer, heart disease and mental health services – the conditions that kill and affect most people will improve with:

- a big expansion in cancer screening programmes

- an end to the postcode lottery in the prescribing of cancer drugs

- rapid access chest pain clinics across the country by 2003

- shorter waits for heart operations

- 335 mental health teams to provide an immediate response to crises.

Older people use the NHS more than any other group. This Plan will provide them with both better and new services:

- national standards for caring for older people to ensure that ageism is not tolerated

- breast screening to cover all women aged 65 to 70 years

- personal care plans for elderly people and their carers

- nursing care in nursing homes to become free

- by 2004 a £900 million package of new intermediate care services to allow older people to live more independent lives

The NHS Plan will bring health improvements across the board for patients but for the first time there will also be a national inequalities target. To help achieve this we will:

- increase and improve primary care in deprived areas

- introduce screening programmes for women and children

- step up smoking cessation services

- improve the diet of young children by making fruit freely available in schools for 4-6 year olds.

The NHS Plan will require investment and reform to make it work. But the funding is there to support change and it is backed by the key organisations in the NHS. There is a new national alliance behind a reformed, patient-centred NHS. These are the most fundamental and far reaching reforms the NHS has seen since 1948.

Introduction by the Secretary of State

For fifty or more years the NHS has been part and parcel of what it means to be British.

For the Government the ideal of the NHS, the way it is funded, remains good today.

We make that case not out of nostalgia, though we are deeply proud of the NHS; not out of dogma, because we have looked at alternative systems and rejected them, but out of conviction: that to make employers and workers pay for healthcare as in France or Germany, or to leave it to the market as in the United States are all recipes for an unfair system and too great a burden on British families and businesses. We should be proud that in Britain we have a fair and efficient model of healthcare.

In the Budget, and confirmed in the spending review, we demonstrated our commitment to the NHS with sustained investment. The NHS budget will grow by one half in cash terms and by one third in real terms over just five years. Decades of under-investment and run-down services are at last being reversed.

By delivering the largest ever sustained increase in NHS funding, the Government has moved the debate from resources to reform. For too long lack of money became an excuse for lack of modernisation. There is now a much wider understanding that the problems of the NHS are more than financial. And now, with the funding issue settled for the next few years, the NHS can address the need to reform itself – from top to toe – to meet the challenges of rising patient expectations.

Over the past four months, specialist teams involving front-line staff, professional groups, patient representatives – alongside senior doctors, nurses and managers – have been helping to prepare this NHS Plan. We have heard from both patients and the public. I am grateful to all of them for their personal contribution to reforming the NHS.

At its heart the problem for today's NHS is that it is not sufficiently designed around the convenience and concerns of the patient. The NHS provides many patients with a good and reliable service. But it is simply not responsive enough to their needs. Patients have to wait too long for treatment. Records get lost. Wards are not clean. Standards are too variable. Old-fashioned demarcations between staff, restricted opening and operating times, outdated systems, unnecessarily complex procedures and a lack of training all combine to create a culture where the convenience of the patient can come a poor second to the convenience of the system.

This is not because staff are lazy or uncaring. Quite the reverse. NHS staff are the biggest asset the health service has. Overwhelmingly they do a brilliant job. But they feel as frustrated with the system as patients do. They have to fight the failings in the system rather than being able to harness its strengths. This is because the NHS is a 1940s system operating in a twenty first century world.

This NHS Plan sets out the steps we now need to take to transform the health service so that it is redesigned around the needs of patients. It means tackling the toughest issues that have been ducked for too long.

For the first time there will be a system of inspection and accountability for all parts of the NHS. The principle will be national standards combined with far greater local autonomy, with new money to reward good performance.

For the first time there will be a consultant contract that gives most money to the doctors working hardest in the NHS.

For the first time nurses and other health professionals will be given the bigger roles that their qualifications and expertise deserve.

For the first time local health services and local social services will be brought closer together in one organisation.

For the first time the NHS and the private sector will work more closely together not just to build new hospitals but to provide NHS patients with the operations they need.

For the first time patients will have an advocate in every hospital, so that a system designed around patients is a system with more power for patients.

These major reforms, we believe, will deliver real benefits for NHS patients: less waiting; faster, more convenient care; improvements in elderly care services and for the top priorities of cancer, heart disease and mental health; visible improvements in the basics of cleaning and food and a new focus on prevention and tackling health inequalities. None of this can be done without many more professionals – and it takes time to train and recruit these staff. Stage by stage – not all at once – patients will see the benefits of these reforms. The timetable and outputs we expect are set out in the National Plan. Expanding and reforming the NHS takes time. Change of this nature and on this scale cannot happen overnight. Others will take time. This is a ten year Plan for reform. But over the next few years patients will see major improvements in their local health services.

This is a once in a lifetime opportunity to bring about the most fundamental and far-reaching reforms the NHS has seen since it was created. This Plan has helped forge a new national alliance behind a modernised NHS.

Reform is backed by large and sustained levels of funding and a Government with the will to see change through.

It is backed by a new consensus in the NHS amongst all the leading health organisations, that this is the best chance for reform.

Over the next few years all of us – the alliance that has come together to build this Plan – must put our energies now into delivering the Plan, so that each year the new milestones are met. Each year, patients will begin to see a new NHS unfolding, growing and getting better, more convenient with less waiting for themselves and their families.

Like key stakeholders, the Government is committed to the NHS core principles set out at the begining of this Plan. Together with all those who share our vision, we will work day in and day out to make it happen.

The Rt Hon. Alan Milburn MP
Secretary of State for Health

1

Our vision: a health service designed around the patient

Introduction

1.1 The vision of this NHS Plan is to offer people fast and convenient care delivered to a consistently high standard. Services will be available when people require them, tailored to their individual needs.

1.2 Our vision is of an NHS where staff are not rushed off their feet and constantly exhausted; where careers are developed not stagnant; where staff are paid properly for good performance; and where childcare is provided in every hospital. Ours is a vision of a renewed public service ethos, a system that values the dedication of staff and believes that trust is still the glue that binds the NHS together.

1.3 It will take time to realise this vision. Step by step over the next ten years the NHS must be redesigned to be patient centred – to offer a personalised service. It is already happening in some places – by 2010 it will be commonplace.

Preventive care

1.4 Routine screening will be extended to cover more conditions. The action patients need to take to minimise the risks to their health – which may have been identified using conventional tests or the new genetic tests that will be increasingly available – will be discussed and agreed with GPs and nurses. The NHS will harness the benefits of advances in genetic technology for the benefits of all.

1.5 The NHS will be at the forefront of assessing new medicines and getting them into use more quickly. It will provide a growing range of products and services to help people adopt healthier lifestyles. As well as drugs to help keep down blood pressure and cholesterol levels, advice on diet and exercise will be accepted as a routine service at the local surgery. The NHS will work with other agencies to tackle the underlying causes of ill health.

1.6 Primary care trusts will identify and maintain registers of those at the greatest risk from serious illness – concentrating particularly on areas where ill health is most prevalent – so that people can be offered preventive treatment. In the process the NHS will help tackle health inequalities.

1.7 NHS Direct nurses will be in regular contact to help patients manage their medicines and check that older people living alone are all right.

1.8 NHSplus will provide an occupational health service to thousands of employers as well as NHS staff themselves.

Self care

1.9 The frontline in healthcare is the home. Most healthcare starts with people looking after themselves and their families at home. The NHS will become a resource which people routinely use every day to help look after themselves. 0845 46 47 will become one of the best used phone numbers as millions of people every year contact NHS Direct to get advice about health problems. Each week will see millions of hits on the NHS Direct internet site. As well as providing fast and reliable information on a wide range of conditions, it will also be valued as an easy way to contact patient and self-help groups.

1.10 The digital TV revolution will enable people to tune into channels dedicated to health issues, with the NHS using its expertise and experience to kitemark the best materials. A new service, NHSplus, will provide information for publication as well as broadcast. And professional training will have much more emphasis on supporting self-care, particularly to help people manage chronic conditions.

Primary care

1.11 A single phone call to NHS Direct will provide a one-stop gateway to healthcare, to give patients more choice about accessing the NHS. Depending on the problem, NHS Direct nurses will advise on care at home, going to the local pharmacist, making a routine appointment, arranging for an emergency consultation, calling an ambulance or social services support. If the problem is routine, NHS Direct will offer the option of ordering the prescription and arrange for delivery to the patient's door. Patients will also have the choice of e-mailing or phoning their practice nurse or GP for advice and booking their appointment online and receiving test results at home. Equally patients, such as the elderly or those that have chronic conditions, will be able to have a continuing relationship with their GP providing continuity of care.

1.12 Round the clock medical care for minor ailments and accidents will be available for all within convenient travelling distance. Ambulances will be equipped with video and monitoring equipment so that victims of accidents can get the most appropriate care while they are being taken to hospital. As services are modernised long waits in accident and emergency departments will become a thing of the past.

1.13 Electronic patient records – to which patients hold a key – will enable nurses, therapists and doctors to maintain continuity of care and knowledge of their patients.

1.14 Many GPs will be working in teams from modern multi-purpose premises alongside nurses, pharmacists, dentists, therapists, opticians, midwives and social care staff. Nurses will have new opportunities and some GPs will tend to specialise in treating different conditions. The consulting room will become the place where appointments for outpatients and operations are booked, test results received and more diagnosis carried out using video and tele-links to hospital specialists. An increasing number of consultants will take outpatient sessions in local primary care centres.

Hospital care

1.15 Changes in primary care will help ease the pressure on hospitals so that they can concentrate on providing specialist care. Appointments will be pre-booked to suit the patient. Tests and diagnosis will be normally carried out on the same day. The next stage of treatment – if it is needed – will be arranged there and then, before the patient leaves the hospital. Around three-quarters of operations will be carried out on a day case basis with no overnight stay required. Traditional waiting lists for surgery will become a thing of the past. There will be waits of weeks rather than months. The uncertainty of not knowing when your operation will happen will be replaced by the certainty of a booked date. Special one-stop diagnosis and treatment centres will concentrate on performing operations, not coping with emergencies.

1.16 Where patients have the most complex illnesses and conditions, such as the need for a heart operation, they will be referred to centres with the best equipment and the staff with the most appropriate expertise – even if that means travelling to a specialist centre.

1.17 There will be a new generation of state of the art hospitals. The old Nightingale wards will be phased out, and more intimate ward bays or rooms will become the norm for those requiring an overnight stay. Day case patients will have comfortable lounges in which to recover. Senior sisters – 'modern matrons' – will have the authority to make sure wards are kept clean and that the basics of care are right for the patient. There will be a Patient Advocate and Liaison Service in every hospital to resolve complaints and concerns quickly. Hospital menus will offer a range of attractive choices throughout the day and the quality of the food served will be checked by hospital nutritionists. There will be a personal bedside TV and telephone for every patient.

Intermediate care

1.18 A new range of intermediate care services will build a bridge between hospital and home, by helping people recover and resume independent living more quickly. This will speed up discharge from hospital when patients are ready to leave. The new services will give older people more independence rather than being forced to choose a care home.

1.19 Intermediate care may be provided in a hospital where, for example, intensive rehabilitation after a stroke is needed. If nursing support is needed nursing homes will be well-placed to offer this service. NHS nursing care will be free. Often people will choose to go home secure in the knowledge they will get the social and health support they need.

1.20 Rapid response and hospital-at-home teams will work on an integrated basis with GPs, community nurses, physiotherapists and social care staff to make sure that people get active support to remain independent at home. New technology in the home will make independent living easier for people who are elderly or disabled.

Quality of care

1.21 People will have the reassurance that the NHS is adopting high standards and striving continuously to improve the quality of its care. Every hospital, primary and community care service and nursing home will issue an annual prospectus setting out its standards, performance and the views of its patients. The funding received by local NHS organisations will be based in part on the results of regular patient surveys.

1.22 National standards for treating all the major conditions will have been established. Appropriate drugs and treatments which are shown to be clinically and cost effective will be in use in every part of the country. Doctors, therapists and nurses will increasingly work to standard protocols. There will be independent inspection of NHS organisations.

Progress so far

1.23 Nothing as ambitious as this vision can be achieved overnight. Putting right decades of neglect and under-investment is a huge task. During the last three years the Government has started to put in place the essential building blocks for a modern NHS. Progress has been made but there is much more still to do.

1.24 The decline in the condition of the NHS estate has been halted. The biggest ever hospital building programme is under way. Every accident and emergency department that needs it and 1,000 GP surgeries are being modernised.

1.25 The extra staff, without which it will be impossible to provide improved services, are also being recruited and trained. There are now over 5,000 more nurse training places and over 1,000 more medical school places in the pipeline than in 1997. There are 10,000 extra qualified nurses and 4,780 more doctors working in the NHS than in 1997.

1.26 The number of treatments the NHS carries out is also rising. Compared to 1997 there are over 500,000 more operations a year, 400,000 more patients being seen as first outpatient appointments and 300,000 more emergencies being dealt with every year.

1.27 New services such as NHS Direct and Walk-in Centres have been introduced. Primary care groups and trusts have been set up to provide the basis for GPs and other health professionals to work together to modernise local health services.

1.28 Big steps have been taken to improve the quality of NHS care by introducing national service frameworks and the National Institute for Clinical Excellence and an independent inspectorate – the Commission for Health Improvement.

Conclusion

1.29 Work has already begun to redesign the NHS so that it is built around the needs of the patient. As the next chapter explains, there is a long way to go. The task for this plan is to show how we can bridge the gulf between the reality of the NHS today and the vision of what it should be like tomorrow.

2

The NHS now

- the NHS has achieved a lot
- there are both public and staff concerns
- the NHS has been underfunded for decades
- a 1940s system in a 21st century world

Introduction

2.1   Britain is committed to the National Health Service. Everyone – no matter how much they earn, who they are, how old they are, where they come from or where they live – should have the health care they need from themselves and for their families. Four-fifths of people today say the NHS is critical to British society and the country must do everything it can to maintain it.

NHS achievements

2.2   The NHS has delivered major improvements in the health of our nation. Free at the point of use, the NHS has freed millions of individuals from worry about the costs of falling ill. In the five decades since the NHS was formed quality of life has improved, with people living healthier as well as longer lives. A baby girl born in 1948 could expect to live for 71 years, a boy for 66 years. Today it is 80 years and 75 years. In the years since 1948, the death rates for babies under a year old have fallen from 34 out of every 1,000 births to six per 1,000 today.

2.3   The NHS has been at the centre of a range of pioneering medical and technological breakthroughs. NHS doctors developed the technique on which the modern approach to hip replacement was based. Cataract surgery is an NHS innovation. Hospitals like Papworth, Great Ormond Street, the Freeman Hospital in Newcastle, Addenbrooke's, St James', Leeds and the Royal Marsden are internationally renowned and respected. Today the NHS is still home to international pioneers in the fields of vaccine development, imaging and gene therapy and many other fields of endeavour. The British system of primary care is envied and copied throughout the world.

2.4 The NHS continues to work at the cutting edge of new forms of health services, inventing new ways of meeting patients' needs, with pioneering developments such as NHS Direct, the Commission for Health Improvement and the National Institute for Clinical Excellence.

2.5 The NHS remains one of the fairest health care systems by international standards. The World Health Organisation recently reported that the NHS was performing better than Germany, the United States and Australia. In surveys, Americans, Canadians and Australians are 50% more worried than British people about affording medical care if they became seriously ill. The NHS is effective and efficient at meeting its goals. The NHS gets more and fairer health care for every pound invested than most other health care systems.

The NHS now: a snapshot

On a typical day in the NHS:

- almost a million people visit their family doctor
- 130,000 go to the dentist for a check up
- 33,000 people get the care they need in accident and emergency
- 8,000 people are carried by NHS ambulances
- 1.5 million prescriptions are dispensed
- 2,000 babies are delivered
- 25,000 operations are carried out including 320 heart operations and 125 kidney operations
- 30,000 people receive a free eye test
- District nurses make 100,000 visits

On a typical day in the NHS, there are:

- 90,000 doctors
- 300,000 nurses
- 150,000 healthcare assistants
- 22,000 midwives
- 13,500 radiographers
- 15,000 occupational therapists

- 7,500 opticians

- 10,000 health visitors

- 6,500 paramedics

- 90,000 porters, cleaners and other support staff

- 11,000 pharmacists

- 19,000 physiotherapists

- 24,000 managers

- 105,000 practice staff in GP surgeries

Public views

2.6   Yet for all the support the NHS enjoys there are widespread public concerns about it. Most people in Britain support the NHS and are broadly satisfied with its overall performance. But many people have real and significant concerns. Young people are the most dissatisfied. About a quarter of the public feel dissatisfied overall with the NHS.

2.7   As part of preparing this Plan a major consultation with members of the public and NHS staff was conducted to gauge their views on the NHS. 152,000 members of the public and 58,000 staff wrote in with their views and their ideas for improving the service. Opinion research asked people about their experience of the NHS. The Office for Public Management (OPM) sat down with groups of people who had used the NHS recently and talked through with them in detail their impressions of the NHS and their hopes for its future. OPM also spoke to the many organisations which represent patients to find out what they thought needed to change. A summary of public views from the consultation can be found in Annex 1.

Top ten things the public wanted to see:

- *more and better paid staff* – more doctors, more nurses, more therapists and scientists

- *reduced waiting times* – reductions in waiting overall, for appointments and on trolleys and in casualty

- *new ways of working* – including 'bringing back matron'

- *care centred on patients* – action on cancelled operations, more convenient services

- *higher quality of care* – especially for cancer and heart disease

- *better facilities* – more cleanliness, better food, getting the basics right

- *better conditions for NHS staff* – reward and recognition for the work NHS staff do

- *better local services* – improvements in local hospitals and surgeries

- *ending the postcode lottery* – high quality treatment assured wherever people live

- *more prevention* – better help and information on healthy living

Staff views

2.8   Most of the public's concerns are shared by NHS staff. Staff views on the NHS were vital to the formation of this NHS Plan. Frontline staff were members of the Modernisation Action Teams which helped in the preparation of the Plan. Hundreds of thousands of staff took time to give their views on how to improve the NHS.

NHS staff wanted to see:

- *more staff* – the top priority was more staff and fair pay

- *training* – more training and improved management skills for all staff

- *joined-up working* – more joined-up working with social services at community and primary care levels

- *less bureaucracy* – reduced administration and bureaucracy and improved funding systems

- *prevention* – more action to help prevent ill health

- *working conditions* – better conditions and aids to recruitment and retention, and more flexible working patterns

- *waiting* – like patients, NHS staff want to see a faster NHS

- *care centred on patients* – staff share patient frustration that the system is too focused on its own needs and doesn't properly meet the need of individual patients

- *national variations* – better performance and accountability systems to reduce variations in service across the country

- *autonomy* – local services to have more control over the way they were organised, with less control from Whitehall.

The underlying problems

2.9 In essence the problem is that despite the best efforts of doctors, nurses and other staff the NHS is not sufficiently centred around the needs of individual patients. There are two major reasons why this is the case. First, decades of under-investment and second, because the NHS is a 1940s system operating in a 21st century world.

An under-invested system

2.10 The NHS is too much the product of the era in which it was born. In its buildings, its ways of working, its very culture, the NHS bears too many of the hallmarks of the 1940s. The rest of society has moved on.

2.11 On July 5th 1948, the day the NHS was founded, the high street banks were open between 10am and 3pm. Today, the public has 24 hour access to banking services. In 1948, women formed a third of the workforce. Today, they make up nearly half. We now live in a diverse, multi-cultural society. Family lives, social structures and public expectations have moved on too. In 1948, deference and hierarchy defined the relationships between citizens and services. In an era of mass production needs were regarded as identical and preferences were ignored.

2.12 Today, successful services thrive on their ability to respond to the individual needs of their customers. We live in a consumer age. Services have to be tailor-made not mass-produced, geared to the needs of users not the convenience of producers. The NHS has been too slow to change its ways of working to meet modern patient expectations for fast, convenient, 24 hour, personalised care.

2.13 Staff in the health service have tried to lead change. In many places they are doing just that. Their efforts to modernise services all too often founder on the fault lines in the NHS which are a hangover from the world of 1948.

A lack of national standards

2.14 From its creation in 1948 there were no national NHS standards. The assumption was that standards would rise automatically in all parts of the country. This is changing now with National Service Frameworks (NSFs) and the National Institute for Clinical Excellence (NICE). But for fifty years it was left to individual health authorities (and during the internal market of the 1990s, to individual GP practices) to decide levels and types of treatment. Professional groups in each area conducted their own evaluation about new treatments. The result was a postcode lottery of prescribing and care.

2.15 An absence of clear national standards made planning and deploying resources – including staff numbers and training – more difficult. Health inequalities were compounded by a failure to match provision of services with health needs.

2.16 There is a huge gap between the best and the rest within the NHS. Rates of hip replacement for those aged over 65 vary from 1.5 per 1,000 population in Doncaster to over 4 per 1,000 in Devon. Some hospitals carry out almost 100% of cataract removal operations as day cases, others less than 10%. For many surgical specialties the top 25% of hospitals get nearly double the output from their consultants as the bottom 25%. In the worst hospitals cancelled operations are running at 5%. The best ones have cancellation rates close to zero. Often the poorest services are in the poorest areas with the poorest results. The NHS has been unable to tackle these unacceptable variations because the 1948 settlement left it with inadequate means to drive up performance.

Demarcations between staff

2.17 Old-fashioned demarcations between staff mean some patients see a procession of health professionals – often recounting the same details to the GP, practice nurse, hospital booking clerk, hospital nurse, care assistant, therapist, junior doctor and consultant. Information is not shared and investigations are often repeated. Delay seems designed into the system.

2.18 Unnecessary boundaries exist between the professions which hold back staff from fulfilling their true potential. Three quarters of house officers do two or more basic tasks not specifically requiring medical training. Up to 40% of patients seeing an orthopaedic consultant in outpatients would be better off being treated by a trained physiotherapist in the first instance. These practices frustrate staff and cause longer waits for patients.

A lack of clear incentives

2.19 The NHS currently lacks the incentives many private sector organisations have to improve performance. Until recently there have been precious few incentives in the system to encourage better performance. Worse still there have been perverse incentives which have inhibited improvements.

2.20 The consultant contract provided incentives for hospital doctors as a combination of a flat salary structure plus rewards for those who build up strong academic reputations and a large private practice. There have been few comparable rewards for the hospital doctors who work hardest to improve services and the quality of care for NHS patients. The way family doctors are rewarded today remains largely unchanged from 1948. GP fees and allowances are related to the number of patients registered with them and insufficiently to the services provided and the quality. The GP remuneration system has failed to reward those who take on additional work to make services more responsive and accessible to patients and to relieve pressures on hospitals. The system has not succeeded in getting the right level of primary care services into the poorest areas which need them most.

2.21 The existing incentives for improved performance by NHS organisations are too narrowly focused on efficiency and squeezing more treatment from the same resources. The incentives have not supported quality, patient responsiveness and partnership with local authorities.

2.22 The current system penalises success and rewards failure. A hospital which manages to treat all its patients within 9 or 12 months rather than 18 may be told that 'over performance' means it has been getting too much money and can manage with less next year. By contrast, hospitals with long waiting lists and times may be rewarded with extra money to bail them out – even though the root of the problem may be poor ways of working rather than lack of funding. The NHS has to move from a culture where it bails out failure to one where it rewards success.

Barriers between services

2.23 Rigid institutional boundaries can mean the needs of individual patients come a poor second to the needs of the individual service. On one day in September last year, 5,500 patients aged 75 and over were ready to be discharged but were still in an acute hospital bed: 23% awaiting assessment; 17% waiting for social services funding to go to a care home; 25% trying to find the right care home; and 6% waiting for the right home care package to be organised. Almost three quarters were not getting the care they needed because of poor co-ordination between the NHS and other agencies. This experience is repeated daily throughout the NHS. Partnerships with local authorities have not been as close or effective as they could be. The 1948 fault line between health and social care has inhibited the development of services shaped around the needs of patients.

2.24 The 1948 settlement more or less separated the provision of NHS healthcare from provision by the private sector. There has been an uneasy truce ever since. Patients who wish to pay for their own care are free to do so but that should not prevent the NHS from using spare private health sector capacity to enhance services for NHS patients.

2.25 The wider inability to forge effective partnerships with local government, business and community organisations has inhibited the NHS' ability to prevent ill health and tackle health inequalities. The NHS has done too little to prevent ill health in the first place. The health gap between the better off and the worst off in society has widened in the last 50 years. The gap between health need and health services remains stubbornly wide. The opportunity of good health and good health services has not been as widely available as it should. This fault line too has to be addressed.

A lack of support and intervention

2.26 For too long NHS organisations have been left to sink or swim. There is a tremendous appetite for change in the NHS. What holds back improvement everywhere is lack of time and support to learn from others about what works. The isolation of individual hospitals and primary care services from one another slows the spread of good practice. Good and bad practice are stuck in their own ghettos because there has been no means of meeting the challenge Aneurin Bevan set out in 1948: how to universalise the best.

2.27 Performance has been inhibited by lack of reliable information for clinicians, managers and patients. Data on clinical, primary care and hospital performance is only now being published annually. The NHS is poor at linking related pieces of information, such as prescription to diagnosis, so results can be collated and used nationally to inform practice, monitor and learn from errors. Most GPs are only just now compiling registers of their patients at risk from heart disease.

2.28 Managers cannot compare costs of services or establish how different staff and organisations are delivering different results for patients. Too often they have to rely on outdated or generalised data when commissioning services and allocating resources to frontline staff.

2.29 For 50 years there has been no systematic way of independently assessing NHS performance. Independent inspection was, until the creation of the Commission for Health Improvement, completely lacking.

2.30 A small minority of organisations and individuals within the NHS persistently fail to deliver high standards of care. The instruments for dealing with persistent failure are old-fashioned and inadequate. The NHS needs a system which spots problems early, takes action swiftly and can act decisively. Persistent failure should be met with an escalating scale of sanctions.

Over centralisation

2.31 The relationship between central government and the NHS has veered between command-and-control and market fragmentation. Neither model works. The NHS cannot be run from Whitehall. Standards cannot simply be set locally either. Until the 1990s the NHS was run hierachically with little room for local innovation or independence. In the 1990s the internal market introduced competition but failed to bring improvements. A new model is needed where intervention is in inverse proportion to success.

2.32 Clinicians and managers want the freedom to run local services. They want to be able to shape services around patients' needs. Inspection, incentives, information and intervention, operating under the umbrella of clear national standards, will help reshape services around the patient.

Disempowered patients

2.33 The relationship between service and patient is too hierarchical and paternalistic. It reflects the values of 1940s public services. Patients do not have their own health records or see correspondence about their own healthcare. The complaints system in the NHS is discredited. Patients have few rights of redress when things go wrong.

2.34 The patient's voice does not sufficiently influence the provision of services. Local communities are poorly represented within NHS decision-making structures. Despite many local and national initiatives to alter the relationship between the NHS and the patient, the whole culture is more of the last century than of this. Giving patients new powers in the NHS is one of the keys to unlocking patient-centred services.

An under-invested system

The NHS has suffered from decades of under investment. In the 1940s some even thought the costs of the NHS would fall as the health of the nation improved. Spending has risen over the years – but not by enough to deliver the sort of modern health services our country needs.

UK spending on healthcare has consistently lagged behind other developed countries. Since 1960 Organisation for Economic Co-operation and Development (OECD) countries have on average increased health spending per capita by 5.5% in real terms compared with only 3.6% in the UK.

Between 1979-1997 the average annual increase in Government spending on health was even less – just 2.9%. And real terms funding in England has veered between under 0% and over 6% a year. This erratic pattern of spending has impeded planning for the shorter, medium and long-term.

As a consequence the NHS has been left with insufficient capacity to provide the services the public expect. England has too few hospital beds per head of population compared with most other health systems. The NHS lacks sufficient doctors, nurses and other skilled staff. There are 1.8 practising doctors per 1,000 people compared with an European Union average of 3.1 per 1,000 population. One third of the buildings used by the NHS today were built before the NHS was even created. The backlog of maintenance in the NHS now stands at £3.1 billion.

The NHS has inadequate levels of modern equipment. IT investment has been too slow and too patchy.

There have been too few operations. In 1995 there were around 360 heart bypass operations per million of the UK population, half of that, for example, in the Netherlands.

Despite its relative efficiency, under investment in the NHS has taken its toll. Too many people wait for treatment and operations. Too many staff are rushed off their feet. Too many hospital buildings appear run down.

The challenge for the NHS

2.35 When the NHS was created it gave Britain a healthcare system in tune with the times. Today its values and principles hold good but NHS practices have become outdated. Too much of what the NHS does and how it does it belongs to a different era. The challenge for the NHS is to prove it can reform its practices to match the high ideals of its principles; to remove the fault lines it inherited from 1948.

2.36 Some say the alternative is to accept the NHS has had its day. To seek a new method of funding healthcare in England. This alternative proposition is examined in the next chapter.

3

Options for funding healthcare

- the public has to pay for healthcare by one means or another
- healthcare systems worldwide are subject to similar pressures as the NHS
- the NHS passes the test of being fair and efficient
- the principles of the NHS are sound. Its practices have to be reformed

Introduction

3.1 There is strong national support for the principles of the NHS even though there are concerns about its practices. There are some who have come to question whether the NHS is sustainable at all. They point to the gap between health need and health services. They point to the apparent advantages of other systems for funding healthcare elsewhere in the world. These critics of the health service say that the time has come to grasp the nettle and abandon the NHS model of care altogether.

3.2 Often the alternative prescriptions for healthcare in our country are presented as simple panaceas, rather than subjected to adequate discussion and analysis. This part of the NHS Plan analyses alternative funding models against the twin tests of efficiency and equity. It concludes that the NHS remains a fair and efficient way of funding healthcare, and that it is the right choice for our country.

Main alternatives

3.3 Essentially those who argue that the NHS is not sustainable advocate making one – or a combination – of four reforms:

- *private insurance:* the Government should incentivise people to make their own arrangements and payments for healthcare in an attempt to ease pressure on the NHS and to seek to raise the total national spend on health.

- *charges:* the Government should introduce new charges for services as an attempt to encourage people to use the health service more responsibly and raise more revenue for the NHS

- *social insurance:* the Government should move wholesale to a French or German style system for funding healthcare where funds are raised predominantly from employees and employers rather than from the population as a whole

- *rationing the service down to a fixed core:* the Government should ration services to a limited list of procedures as a response to medical advance

3.4   Each of these proposals has been examined against two key criteria which should underpin any modern healthcare funding system:

- *efficiency:* testing whether the proposal would achieve its proposed end and whether it provides the greatest possible health improvement and healthcare within the funding available

- *equity:* analysing how well the proposal would match financial contributions to ability to pay, and how well it would match healthcare to health needs.

Private health insurance

3.5   When people propose the Government should boost national spending on health, by incentivising individuals to make provision for their own healthcare needs, they normally mean tax incentives for individuals and/or employers for making contributions towards private medical insurance.

The efficiency test

3.6   This approach is inefficient in five respects:

3.7   First, as a policy its effects are likely to be minimal without a strong element of compulsion. In 1990 the previous Government introduced tax relief on private medical insurance for the over 60s. Despite annual public spending of £140 million on these incentives the numbers of subscribers to private medical insurance rose by only about 50,000 in seven years. This 1.6 % increase therefore had only a marginal effect on the NHS. More recent experience from Australia confirms this analysis. Three years of experimenting with increasingly costly public subsidies – totalling £1 billion – appears to have merely stopped a long term decline in the coverage of private health insurance. These subsidies have mainly benefited those already with insurance and so far may have added much more to public spending than to private funding.[1]

3.8   Second, using public money to pay for tax incentives diverts funds from the public healthcare system. The cost of providing tax relief to those who already have private health insurance would be significantly over £500 million – the so-called dead weight cost. Unless taxes were to rise or spending in another area of government were to fall, that would mean the NHS budget being reduced by the same amount.

3.9 Third, it is misleading to presume that incentives for people to 'go private' saves the public sector money. This is because the saving to the NHS is likely to be outweighed by the 'deadweight' costs of subsidising those who already have private medical insurance. A recent report from the Institute for Fiscal Studies concluded that: "it is extremely unlikely that the cost of any such subsidy to private medical insurance would be less than the NHS expenditure saved"[2]. In other words, switching public funding from NHS expenditure to spending on tax reliefs could reduce health spending overall.

3.10 Fourth, the development of genetic testing will affect the coverage and cost of voluntary private health insurance. Healthcare risks will become more transparent. As a result, premiums will rise to reflect high-risk subscribers' likely claims, reducing the affordability of cover, and lower risk subscribers will drop out. The combined effect will be to erode the risk pool on which private health insurance depends.

3.11 Fifth, whether or not the introduction of tax relief increased the overall volume of healthcare it would certainly inflate its costs:

- *labour costs:* currently there is no surplus of doctors and nurses in our country. The previous Government considered the introduction of tax relief in 1988. As Nigel Lawson, the then Chancellor of the Exchequer, concluded: "If we simply boost demand, for example by tax concessions to the private sector, without improving supply, the result would not be so much a growth in private health care, but higher prices"[3]

- *fragmentation:* the more fragmented commissioning of healthcare becomes, the more prices would be likely to rise. In the USA, for example, pharmaceutical prices are on average 75% higher than in Britain. This is at least in part due to the fragmentation of healthcare purchasing

- *administration:* administrative costs would rise significantly. The costs of management and administration are much higher under private insurance because of the bureaucracy needed to assess risk, set premiums, design complex benefit schedules and review, pay or refuse claims. These raised costs impact on hospital budgets. Administrative costs in America are up to 15% higher than in Canada, largely because of the cost of insurance processing.[4] The implication is that much of any increase in private medical insurance in Britain would go in administrative costs with no direct benefits to patients.

The equity test

3.12 Private medical insurance is inequitable. Subsidising private health insurance will use taxpayers funds to expand two-tier access to healthcare, reducing equitable access to needed care. The costs of private health insurance per individual are substantial. For a 65 year old private health insurance costs around 50% more than the equivalent NHS cost.

3.13 Private medical insurance shifts the burden of paying for health care from the healthy, young and wealthy to the unhealthy, old and poor. The cost of private health insurance rises the older and sicker the person – indeed beyond a certain age, and with chronic conditions, it is virtually impossible to get private insurance cover. Tax relief for private health insurance by definition is regressive. It offers public subsidies to the better off and is meaningless for the worst off.

3.14 This view is borne out by findings from a large scale research study in the early 1990s which looked at the costs across income classes of healthcare in Europe and America. It concluded that: 'the two countries with predominately private financing systems – Switzerland and the US – have the most regressive structures overall... The group of Countries with the next most regressive systems are the countries operating the so-called social insurance model, ...countries which rely...mainly on tax finance... have the least regressive financing systems'.[5]

Charges

3.15 Proponents of patient charges argue that new charges should be introduced for a range of health services to encourage responsible use of resources and raise more revenue for the NHS.

The efficiency test

3.16 Where charges are high they generally reduce service use across the board. The most thorough study of charges and cost-sharing, the RAND Health Insurance Experiment – a randomised trial undertaken in the USA in the 1970s – found that charges led to less use of preventative care[6]. The available evidence suggests that they are also likely to discourage use of necessary services. As the World Health Organisation has recently noted: 'The use of co-payments has the effect of rationing the use of a specific intervention but does not have the effect of rationalising its demand by consumers'.[7] Lower use and delayed access to healthcare services, especially preventive services, may divert demand to more costly parts of the system and may result in higher healthcare costs in the longer term.

3.17 It is sometimes suggested that these undesirable behavioural effects can be avoided by setting new user charges at a low level. Where charges are low they raise very little cash, which may be off-set by administrative and collection costs. For example in 1992 New Zealand introduced charges for the use of hospital beds. The difficulty of collecting the charges from patients led to their rapid abolition in

1993 after only a year[8]. Equally, in countries such as France that make widespread use of charges, many individuals take out supplementary insurance just to pay them, thus defeating the object of introducing the charges at all.

The equity test

3.18 Charges are inequitable in two important respects. First, new charges increase the proportion of funding from the unhealthy, old and poor compared with the healthy, young and wealthy. In particular, high charges risk worsening access to healthcare by the poor. As the World Heath Organisation report – which assessed the United Kingdom as having one of the fairest systems in the world for funding healthcare – concludes: 'Fairness of financial risk protection requires the highest possible degree of separation between contributions and utilisation'.[7]

3.19 Second, exempting low income families from user charges can create inequities for those just above the threshold. High user charges with exemptions can create disincentives to earning and working through the imposition of high marginal tax rates.

3.20 Some European countries do make more use of user charges than Britain. For example, in parts of Sweden in 1996 there were charges for seeing a GP at about £10 per visit and for seeing a consultant of about £20 per consultant[9]. They are able to do so in large part because they tend to compensate people indirectly through the social security benefit system. Even so, in Sweden, there is evidence that user charges for visiting primary care doctors have discouraged people from seeking treatment.[10]

Continental social insurance

3.21 There are those who advocate maintaining the current role of public funding but shifting wholesale to a social insurance-based model. This is similar to both the German and French healthcare systems. The proponents of this model argue that it leads to larger shares of national income going to healthcare.

The efficiency test

3.22 Social insurance systems involve payments from individuals just like tax-financed systems. In the French and German social insurance systems, costs fall predominantly on the employer and employee and so fewer people contribute. An outline estimate from 1997 is that a wholesale switch to funding the NHS predominantly from national insurance contributions would cost an extra £1,000 per employee using the French model of public healthcare funding and about £700 per employee per year using the German model, without any increase in the total amount of resources going to the NHS. These calculations adjust for the different levels of expenditure in the three countries i.e. French and German expenditures are assumed to be reduced to current British levels. At 2003-4 levels of funding, additional costs would be the equivalent of £1,500 per worker per year using the French model and £1,000 using the German model, again, with no addition to currently planned NHS funding.

3.23 Continental social insurance models are less efficient in several respects.

3.24 First, because of the design of the social insurance systems in continental Europe, it is not clear that all of the extra spending is spent efficiently. Cost control under European social insurance systems has been weak because payers have acted as financial intermediaries within the healthcare system but have not played a role in scrutinising the performance, efficiency and effectiveness of the system itself. In the words of the German Head of the Federal Association of General Sick Funds: 'Germany pays for a luxury car but gets a medium-range car in return' and 'if we don't look out, our medium-range car will soon be without brakes and wheels'.[11]

3.25 The French system, despite patient choice, is wasteful in the use of many of its resources. Over-prescribing is common.[12] At only 3%, generic prescribing rates are far lower than the 60% found in Britain. To tackle these inefficiencies France and Germany are turning to healthcare management mechanisms which have been in operation in Britain for many years, such as a GP referral based system of primary care.

3.26 Second, in recent years fiscal policy and competitiveness considerations have forced all governments to subject social insurance systems to increasingly tight regulation. By placing caps on contribution rates or expenditure, the national governments in Germany and France now effectively determine overall expenditure under their social insurance systems rather than the social insurance partners. In other words, levels of health funding are increasingly unrelated to the system of raising finance and increasingly related to how much the economy can afford and the level of priority placed on health spending by the public.

The equity test

3.27 The extent to which social insurance is equitable depends upon the form of the particular scheme.

Rationing to a core service

3.28 The fourth solution sometimes suggested is that the NHS should be restricted or 'rationed' to a defined core of individual conditions or treatments. There are several problems with this suggestion.

3.29   First, advocates of this position usually have great difficulty specifying what they would rule out. The sort of treatments that commonly feature include varicose veins, wisdom teeth extraction or cosmetic procedures. The problem is that these sort of services account for less than 0.5% of the NHS budget, and are not major cost-drivers for the future. Instead, the vast majority of spending – and spending increases – go on childbirth, elderly care, and major conditions such as cancer, heart disease, and mental health problems.

3.30   The second major problem is that different patients under different circumstances often derive differing benefits from the same treatment.

3.31   The NHS is not a system under which each patient only gets a fixed 'ration' of healthcare, regardless of their personal need and circumstances. The fact that a patient has previously been treated for one condition will not of itself prevent her or him from being treated for subsequent conditions. If however 'rationing' merely means that it has never and will never be possible in practice to provide all the healthcare theoretically possible, then it is true of every healthcare system in the world.

3.32   The issue is not *whether* the NHS – just like every other public or private health service – has to set priorities and make choices. The issue is *how* those choices are made. Under the NHS, treatment is based on peoples' ability to benefit. We are in a period of significant expansion of health service resources. The issue is how to improve decisions about how those expanded resources are used. We can no longer leave to chance decisions about how treatment is provided, how demand is managed, and how costs are driven. National Service Frameworks and the broad priorities set out in this NHS Plan provide the context. The National Institute for Clinical Excellence, supported by its new Citizens Council (see paragraph 10.20) will help the NHS to focus its growing resources on those interventions and treatments that will best improve peoples' health. By pointing out which treatments are less clinically cost-effective, it will help free up financial headroom for faster uptake of more appropriate and clinically cost-effective interventions. This is the right way to set priorities: not a crudely rationed core service.

Conclusion

3.33   There is no perfect healthcare system. Systems worldwide are subject to the same sort of pressures facing the NHS. In Germany, for example, there have been four major health reform packages since 1990, and debate continues about the need for further reform. In France, there has been growing disquiet amongst employers about the costs of the social insurance scheme. In the USA, both Presidential contenders, George W. Bush and Al Gore, are proposing major changes to deal with the problem of the over forty million Americans not covered by health insurance.

3.34 No healthcare system is beyond reform and political controversy. But the way that the NHS is financed continues to make sense. It meets the tests of efficiency and equity. The principles on which the NHS was constructed in 1948 remain fundamentally sound. Its practices, sometimes stuck in the world of 1948, need fundamental reform. Investment and reform are the twin solutions to the problems the NHS faces.

References

[1] Hall J, De Abreu Lauenco R, Viney R: *Carrots and Sticks – the Fall and Fall of Private Insurance in Australia, Health Economics Vol. 8 No. 8*, 653-60 December 1999.

[2] Emmerson C, Frayne C, Goodman A, *Pressures in UK Healthcare: Challenges for the NHS, Institute for Fiscal Studies,* London, 2000.

[3] Lawson, Nigel, *The View from No.11: Memoirs of a Tory Radical, London Bantam Press,* 1992.

[4] Woolhandler S, Himmelstein DU and Lewontin JP, *Administrative costs in US hospitals, New England Journal of Medicine, 329(6) 400-3 August 5 1993*

[5] Van Doorslaer E, Wagstaff A, and Rutten F (eds), *Equity in the Finance and Delivery of Healthcare: An International Perspective, Oxford University Press,* 1993.

[6] Lurie N, Manning W G, Peterson C, Goldberg G A, Phelps C A, Lillard L, *Preventative care: do we practise what we preach?, American Journal of Public Health, 77(7), 801-4,* July 1987.

[7] World Health Organisation, *The World Health Organisation Report 2000, Health Systems: Improving Performance, WHO,* Geneva, 2000.

[8] Stocks P, *Changes to health targeting, Social Policy Journal of New Zealand, 1 60-73* November 1993.

[9] Anell A, Svarvar P, *Health care reforms and cost containment in Sweden,* in Mossialos E and Le Grand J, eds. *Health Care and Cost Containment in the European Union,* Aldershot, Ashgate, 1999.

[10] Elofsson S, Unden AL, Krakau I, *Patient charges – a hindrance to financially and psychosocially disadvantaged groups seeking care, Social Science and Medicine, 46(10) 1375-80 May 1998*

[11] *"Germany pays for a luxury car, but gets a medium-range car in return"* and *"if we don't look out, our medium-range car will soon be without brakes and wheels"* – Hans Jurgen Ahrens quoted in Suddeutsche Zeitung, 17/18 June 2000

[12] *The French system, despite patient choice, is wasteful in the use of many of its resources. Over-prescribing is common* – OECD, Economic Survey 1999-200, France OECD, Paris, 2000

4

Investing in NHS facilities

- 7,000 extra beds in hospitals and intermediate care
- over 100 new hospitals by 2010
- 500 new one-stop primary care centres
- over 3,000 GP premises modernised
- 250 new scanners
- modern IT in every hospital and GP surgery
- clean wards, better food

Introduction

4.1   The NHS has been under funded for decades. Now there will be sustained investment. The funding announced in this year's Budget means the NHS in England will benefit from annual average real terms growth of 6.3% – twice the historic growth rate. The NHS budget will grow by around one half in cash terms and one third in real terms in just five years.

Net England NHS expenditure in real terms (based on 1997 – 1998 prices)

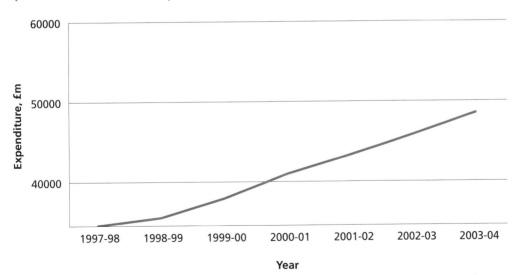

4.2   As the first priority this scale of investment will be used to get the basics right in the health service – the right number and the right type of beds, buildings, services and equipment – alongside the right number of staff.

4.3   We will use this unprecedented investment to modernise NHS services around the needs of patients.

New beds

4.4   The National Beds Inquiry confirmed that the NHS does not have the right beds in the right places to do its job quickly and effectively.

Shaping the future NHS: responses to the National Beds Inquiry

The National Beds Inquiry Consultation invited members of the public and professionals to tell the Government what pattern of services the NHS should provide in the future, focusing on services for older people as the main users of hospital services. More than 5,000 copies of the National Beds Inquiry were requested and 8 Listening Events were held. Around 450 written responses were received from a wide range of sources including individuals, primary care groups, health authorities, trusts, royal colleges, doctors, nurses, other health service professionals, academics, local councils, community health councils, unions, charities, private companies and other representative organisations.

Respondents envisaged a service that would be more 'joined-up' with patients moving along tailored care pathways and no discernible divide between the different elements of the health and social care system. In particular:

• there was near universal support for development of 'care closer to home'

• in the short- and medium-term, however, the majority felt that there was a need to at least maintain adequate numbers of acute beds

• there was a need to radically integrate the way the NHS works with social services

• the majority of the respondents wanted to create a 24-hour a day 7 day a week 365 day a year integrated health and social service system focused on the patient

• this new service should be based around the key themes of patient empowerment and education of the public

• prevention of disease and early intervention in the community would be of fundamental importance.

Respondents saw the use of intermediate care as central to this more joined-up approach. It should concentrate on maintaining and restoring independence, and on rehabilitation. It would act as a bridge between community and hospital care. Both staff and patients would experience new ways of working which would blur the

boundary between primary and secondary care. Specific elements of this new
service would include:

- non-appointment 'drop in' facilities

- fast access to diagnostics and pathology leading to effective interventions

- multi-disciplinary teams focused on particular groups and conditions

- a mix of nurse, therapist, consultant and GP led services

- fast access to acute settings where needed

- access to non-acute inpatient settings where appropriate

- timely discharge into appropriate settings.

Within this new service a new generation of staff including specialist GPs, multi-skilled
workers, geriatricians, nurses, social workers and professions allied to medicine would
apply their particular skills in both acute and community settings. The private and
voluntary sector would have important roles to play. This new environment would be
supported by electronic patient records and a fuller use of new technologies.

Although much of the National Beds Inquiry was focused on the particular needs of
older people, the majority of respondents also felt that other patient groups would
benefit from a similar joined up approach.

As a result of this Plan there will be:

- 7,000 extra NHS beds by 2004

- of these around 2,100 extra beds will be in general and acute wards. This will be
  the first increase of its kind in 30 years

- 5,000 extra intermediate care beds, some in community or cottage hospitals,
  others in specially designated wards in acute hospitals. Some will be in purpose
  built new facilities or in redesigned private nursing homes

- 1,700 extra non-residential intermediate care places

- a 30% increase in adult critical care beds over the next 3 years as a result of
  resources allocated this year and to follow over the next three years.

These increases in beds and places, especially for older people, should help improve bed
availability levels in hospitals.

4.5 Clear guidelines will be issued on likely future requirements for beds and types of services which should be available in all areas. Future capital developments will need to demonstrate they have taken full account of these guidelines before they receive funding.

New hospitals

4.6 There will be major investment in new NHS buildings. The biggest ever hospital building programme in the history of the NHS is already underway. We have given the go ahead to 38 major developments. Over half of these will be open to the public by 2003/04 and the remainder will be under construction. In addition, we have given the go ahead to a further 31 medium size schemes of which 27 will be open.

4.7 As a result of this NHS Plan there will now be a further major expansion in new hospital building:

- 9 new hospital schemes given the go ahead in 2001 – worth £1.3billion

- 9 new hospital schemes given the go ahead in 2002 – worth £1billion

- this will mean over 100 new hospital schemes in total between 2000 and 2010.

4.8 Capital investment will also reshape services. In partnership with the private sector we will develop a new generation of Diagnostic and Treatment Centres to increase the number of elective operations which can be treated in a single day or with a short stay. These Centres will separate routine hospital surgery from hospital emergency work so they can concentrate on getting waiting times down. As a result of this NHS Plan there will be:

- 20 Diagnostic and Treatment Centres developed by 2004. By then, 8 will be fully operational treating approximately 200,000 patients a year.

New NHS buildings

4.9 As well as new hospitals there will be a range of other new buildings developed between 2000 and 2010. As a result of the NHS Plan there will be:

- £7 billion of new capital investment through an extended role for PFI by 2010

- 40% of the total value of the NHS estate will be less than fifteen years old by 2010

- the NHS will have cleared at least a quarter of its £3.1 billion maintenance backlog, accumulated through two decades of under-investment, by 2004

- up to £600 million realised through a one-off auction of empty and surplus NHS property to reinvest in new NHS premises.

4.10   The new buildings will be provided through a mixture of public capital and an extended role for the Private Finance Initiative. Where there is a major PFI deal to build a new hospital taking place, we will, when appropriate, include local NHS primary and intermediate redevelopment too. In this way we will help ensure that capital investment is contributing to the redesign of local services across a whole health economy.

New local surgeries

4.11   The NHS will enter into a new public private partnership within a new equity stake company – the NHS Local Improvement Finance Trust (NHS Lift) – to improve primary care premises in England. The priority will be investment in those parts of the country – such as the inner cities – where primary care services are in most need of expansion. As a result of this NHS Plan:

- up to £1 billion will be invested in primary care facilities

- up to 3,000 family doctors' premises will be substantially refurbished or replaced by 2004.

4.12   This record investment will allow for a range of brand new types of NHS facilities, bringing primary and community services – and where possible social services – together under one roof to make access more convenient for patients. New one-stop primary care centres will include GPs, dentists, opticians, health visitors, pharmacists and social workers. As a result of this NHS Plan there will be:

- 500 one-stop primary care centres by 2004.

New equipment

4.13   After decades of under-investment there is a crying need for new NHS equipment. We will make real progress by investing over £300 million in equipment to improve cancer, renal and heart disease services by 2004:

- 50 new Magnetic Resonance Imaging (MRI) cancer scanners to increase procedures by 190,000

- 200 new CT cancer scanners – 150 replacement plus 50 additional – to increase procedures by 240,000

- 80 new liquid cytology units to improve cervical cancer screening for 4 million patients every year

- 45 new linear accelerators – 20 replaced plus 25 additional – to treat an extra 12,000 cancer patients

- 3,000 new automated defibrillators in public places to help save the lives of the one in five people whose heart attacks happen in a public place.

- 450 new and replacement haemodialysis stations to treat another 1,850 kidney patients and provide better treatment for a further 1,200 existing patients.

Clean hospitals

4.14 The new investment we are making will allow the NHS to get the basics right. Patients perceive a major deterioration in the cleanliness of hospitals since the introduction of Compulsory Competitive Tendering and the internal market. Patients expect wards to be clean, furnishings to be tidy. The new resources will allow for a renewed emphasis on clean hospitals.

4.15 As a result of this NHS Plan there will be:

- over £30 million allocated immediately direct to hospital trusts to improve hospital cleaning. In future years, cash for cleaning will be distributed as part of the normal allocation process

- a nation-wide clean-up campaign throughout the NHS starting immediately. All patient areas, visitor toilets, outpatients and accident and emergency units will be thoroughly cleaned and kept clean. Chairs, linen, pillows, furniture, floor coverings and blinds which are dirty will be cleaned. Those beyond repair will be replaced

- every hospital will have an unannounced inspection of its cleanliness, by a specialist inspection team including patients within the next 6 months. The results will be made available to the local media

- national standards for cleanliness will form part of the NHS Performance Assessment Framework. Every hospital's performance will be measured against these standards by the end of 2000

- ward sisters and charge nurses will have the authority to ensure the wards they lead are properly cleaned. Hospital domestics will be fully part of the ward team – and respected for the important work they do

- NHS trusts will have to adjust contracts with external cleaning companies to ensure nurses can take the lead in ensuring wards are properly cleaned where necessary

- every NHS trust will nominate a Board member to take personal responsibility for monitoring hospital cleanliness, and will report to the Board following regular check ups. The Patients' Forum in each trust will monitor standards and use unannounced inspections to do this

- the independent NHS watchdog, the Commission for Health Improvement, will inspect and report on this aspect of NHS care.

Better hospital food

4.16   The NHS provides over 300 million meals each year at a cost of £500 million. The food is variable in quality, it is not provided in a way which is sufficiently responsive to patients, and too much of it is wasted as a result. These standards are not good enough.

4.17   As a result of this NHS Plan by 2001 there will be:

- a 24-hour NHS catering service with a new NHS menu, designed by leading chefs. It will cover continental breakfast, cold drinks and snacks at mid-morning and in the afternoon, light lunchtime meals and an improved two-course evening dinner. This will be a minimum standard for all hospitals

- a national franchise for NHS catering will be examined to ensure hospital food is provided by organisations with a national reputation for high quality and customer satisfaction

- half of all hospitals will have new 'ward housekeepers' in place by 2004 to ensure that the quality, presentation and quantity of meals meets patient needs; that patients, particularly elderly people, are able to eat the meals on offer; and that the service patients receive is genuinely available round-the-clock

- dieticians will advise and check on nutritional values in hospital food. Patients' views will be measured as part of the Performance Assessment Framework and there will be unannounced inspections of the quality of hospital food.

4.18   An extra £10 million a year will be made available to deliver these improvements in hospital food.

At Nottingham City Hospital, a ward waitress reports to the ward manager, taking orders from the patient, and ensuring they get something suitable to eat. The introduction of this service has dramatically reduced food wastage by 40%. The waitress has opportunities for NVQ qualification in nutrition and silver service. As well as serving the food, and reporting to the nursing staff on each patient's food intake, she can provide tempting snack alternatives from the ward kitchen, at times to suit the patient.

Bedside televisions and telephones

4.19 In an age of cable and digital TV, with over half the population owning mobile phones, people increasingly expect to have access to these services wherever they are. It is no longer acceptable for patients to have to wait for a nurse to wheel a trolley to their bed or have to stand in a draughty corridor if they want to make a call. With the new resources, the NHS can do much more to provide better facilities at the bedside.

4.20 A number of hospitals have already negotiated contracts with a private company to install bedside TVs and phones. There are modest charges for the service – though normally there are no charges on children's wards. Patients are able to make outgoing calls at a level below the standard national call rate. They can also watch videos and one of the channels is dedicated to use by the hospital to show programmes that will help patients prepare for their operation or to explain aspects of their treatment. As a result of this NHS Plan:

- The contract to extend this service nationwide will be advertised by the autumn

- Bedside televisions and telephones will be available in every major hospital by 2004.

New information technology

4.21 The NHS will have the most up-to-date information technology systems to deliver services faster and more conveniently for patients. We are already investing £200 million in modernising IT systems. As a result of this NHS Plan there will be:

- an extra £250 million invested in information technology in 2003/04

- electronic booking of appointments for patient treatment by 2005

- access to electronic personal medical records for patients by 2004. By then 75% of hospitals and 50% of primary and community trusts will have implemented electronic patient record systems. When the necessary infrastructure has been put in place, and we have fully evaluated technical feasibility on effectiveness, smart cards for patients allowing easier access to health records will be introduced

- electronic prescribing of medicines by 2004 giving patients faster and safer prescibing as well as easier access to repeat prescriptions

- all GP practices will be connected to NHSnet by 2002, giving patients improved diagnosis, information and referral

- through investment in electronic patient records all local health services will have facilities for telemedicine by 2005 allowing patients to connect with staff electronically for advice.

4.22 NHS staff will also benefit from the investment in new information technology. Staff will get easy access to up-to-date and accurate information on patients' medical histories. NHS staff will be able to order tests, refer patients and make bookings of appointments for patients using new IT. The National Electronic Library for Health will provide electronic access to state-of-the-art information on latest treatments and best practice. This investment will allow for greater efficiency and also for easier access to the information necessary to monitor local performance and practices against national standards and performance indicators.

Conclusion

4.24 The new resources will allow the NHS to get the basics right. Not everything can be put right overnight – the decades of neglect make that impossible. But over the next few years the NHS will start to look and feel like a different place. There will be better, more modern facilities both for patients and for staff.

5

Investing in NHS staff

- 7,500 more consultants and 2,000 more GPs
- 20,000 extra nurses and over 6,500 extra therapists
- 1,000 more medical school places on top of the 1,100 already anounced
- extra pay in shortage areas and a new pay system for all staff
- more childcare support for staff, with 100 on-site nurseries
- improvements in occupational health and the working environment

Introduction

5.1 NHS staff are a precious resource. They are what make the NHS tick. A modern NHS must offer staff a better deal in their working lives. It is never an easy life working in the NHS but it can be a better life. This chapter and chapters eight and nine, set out the improvements we will make. Our task is not just to end years of underfunding. It is to end years of low morale.

5.2 The biggest constraint the NHS faces today is no longer shortage of financial resources. It is shortage of human resources – the doctors, nurses, therapists and other health professionals who keep the NHS going day-in and day-out.

5.3 It takes years to train doctors, nurses, therapists and other health professionals. Our ability to expand the NHS workforce is still being constrained by the limited investment made by the previous government in education and training for the future of the NHS. Within these constraints, there will now be an unparalleled increase in the number of key staff over the next four years.

More staff

5.4 Between now and 2004 there will be:

- 7,500 more consultants

- 2,000 more general practitioners

- 20,000 more nurses

- over 6,500 more therapists and other health professionals.

5.5 These are very challenging targets but we must meet them – and, if possible, exceed them – if the NHS is to make the service gains for patients they need. We will achieve them by:

- increasing throughput from training

- modernising pay structures and increasing earnings

- improving the working lives of staff

- recruiting more staff from abroad.

More training places

5.6 By 2004, on current plans, we expect more than 45,000 new nurses and midwives to come out of training and over 13,000 therapists and other health professionals. Now we can go further. There will be further year on year increases in the number of training places available for all health professionals.

5.7 As a result of this NHS Plan there will be:

- 5,500 more nurses, midwives and health visitors being trained each year by 2004, than today

- 4,450 more therapists and other key professional staff being trained by 2004

- 1,000 more specialist registrars – the key feeder grade for consultants – by 2004, targeting key specialties. This will deliver a further acceleration in the numbers of consultants later in the decade

- 450 more doctors training for general practice by 2004.

New medical school places

5.8 1,000 of the 1,100 extra medical school places the Government has already announced are expected to come on stream by 2002. We need to build on this progress with a further major expansion in numbers to be delivered by 2005. As a result of this NHS Plan:

- we will seek a further increase in the number of medical school places of up to 1,000 – as a result the number of medical students will have increased by up to 40% since 1997, the biggest rise in a generation.

Improved pay for NHS staff

5.9   The public want to see better, fairer rewards for NHS staff. The Government shares this ambition. For the last two years pay awards recommended by the independent pay review bodies have been implemented in full. Since 1997 nurses have had a 15% pay rise. We have agreed, in principle, a new system of intensity payments for consultants to reflect increasing workloads and negotiated a new contract for doctors in training to give more rewards to those working most intensively and doing the most anti-social hours. We have agreed an above-inflation pay rise for staff outside the Review Body, not just for one year but for three years.

5.10   We are prepared to invest in pay. We also know the current NHS pay system inhibits the modernisation of the service. It has failed to keep pace with changes in NHS practice, and does not recognise that modern forms of healthcare rely on flexible teams of staff working across traditional skill boundaries. The NHS needs a new pay system – one that rewards staff for what they do, for their own particular skills and abilities, rather than simply being based on their job title. We will continue our discussions with the organisations who represent staff on delivering these goals. We will shortly publish a joint document reporting on progress and setting out the future timetable. In the meantime we will make progress on two fronts.

5.11   First, the contribution midwives make to the lives of mothers and babies has long been recognised by the population. It has not been sufficiently recognised within the NHS pay system. As a result of this NHS Plan the Government will act immediately to ensure that midwives with a year's satisfactory service will have access to progression from the top three pay points of Grade E to the top of Grade F without the need for promotion.

5.12   Second, we will move quickly to increase incentives for staff to join or re-join the NHS in those parts of the country where labour shortages are most serious. As part of the current negotiations on pay, the Government is considering a more flexible system capable of responding to different pressures in local labour markets within a national framework. As part of this NHS Plan the Government proposes a new Market Forces Supplement to top up the pay of staff in areas where there are labour market shortages.

5.13   There will be more help with accommodation costs, including the provision of affordable, good quality modern houses and flats for nurses and other staff. We will evaluate the concept of staff hotels to accommodate the significant numbers of staff who travel into city centre hospitals and whose working patterns make travel between work and home difficult. We will provide 2,000 extra units of nurse accommodation in London within the next three years. A detailed analysis of nurse accommodation needs outside London, particularly in the South East, will be completed by the autumn.

Improving Working Lives

5.14 Improving the working lives of staff contributes directly to better patient care through improved recruitment and retention – and because patients want to be treated by well-motivated, fairly rewarded staff. We have shown over the last 18 months that intensive action to bring back professionals into the NHS can succeed. Since February 1999 over 4,000 nurses and midwives have already returned to work in the NHS, and over 2,000 more are preparing to do so. But we have to go further and faster. That means extending the national recruitment campaign to other staff groups and intensifying follow-up action, with more – and more accessible – return to practice courses, a willingness across the board to offer flexible working practices, and effective support and mentoring of newly returned staff.

5.15 As a result of this NHS Plan, for the first time, the way NHS employers treat staff will be part of the core performance measures and linked to the financial resources they receive. Therefore:

- a new Performance Framework for Human Resources will be published immediately, incorporated into the overall Performance Assessment Framework

- all NHS employers will be assessed against performance targets and a new Improving Working Lives (IWL) Standard

- by April 2003 all NHS employers are expected to be accredited as putting the Improving Working Lives standard into practice.

5.16 The Improving Working Lives standard means that every member of staff in the NHS is entitled to belong to an organisation which can prove that it is investing in their training and development, tackling discrimination and harassment, improving diversity, applying a zero tolerance on violence against staff, reducing workplace accidents, reducing sick absences, providing better occupational health and counselling services, conducting annual attitude surveys – asking relevant questions and acting on the key messages. Standards and targets have already been established to support these goals. It is now down to NHS employers to deliver them. As a result of the NHS Plan we will give their efforts a further impetus.

5.17 We will ensure more help with personal development and training: by investing an extra £140 million by 2003/04 to ensure that all professional staff are supported in keeping their skills up to date and to provide access to learning for all NHS staff without a professional qualification.

5.18 An extra £9 million – £25,000 for every NHS trust – will be provided immediately, to go into tangible, practical improvements in the working environment for staff and to be spent as staff themselves want – whether on providing a face-lift to staff rooms or improving other basic facilities – based on responses to the local annual staff survey or other means of staff involvement.

5.19 We will invest an additional £6 million in 2001/02 building to £8m in 2003/04, to extend occupational health services, already a requirement in hospitals and community trusts, to GPs and their staff. Standards for occupational health services for NHS staff will be included in the Improving Working Lives standard.

5.20 Under the Improving Working Lives standard every member of staff in the NHS is also entitled to work for an organisation which can demonstrate its commitment to more flexible working conditions: challenging traditional working patterns and giving staff more control over their own time; one which provides team-based employee-led rostering, annual hours arrangements, childcare support, reduced hours options, flexi-time, career support, career breaks and flexible retirement. Staff should themselves be involved in the design and development of better working practices and in decisions which affect their working lives. The standard and the associated performance improvement and monitoring framework means this will no longer be left to chance.

5.21 In addition, to boost childcare arrangements and expand NHS sponsored and on-site nursery provision, we will now earmark extra funding, building up to an additional investment of over £30million by 2004. As a result of the NHS Plan:

- by 2004 there will be provision for on-site nurseries at around 100 hospitals provided at an average subsidy of £30 per place per week

- every NHS trust will have a child-care co-ordinator to be the parent's advocate and adviser also available to primary care groups and primary care trusts. They will co-ordinate the provision of nursery places and a network of secure provision for school-aged children drawing on after school clubs, local childminding networks and holiday play schemes to meet local needs

- from now a requirement for the provision of on-site nursery and child-care facilities will be built into all plans for new NHS hospitals; and we will review existing commissions to ensure that they make satisfactory provision for such facilities.

International recruitment

5.22   To further boost NHS staff numbers in the short term, the Department of Health will work with the leaders of the professions and with other government departments to recruit additional suitably qualified staff from abroad where this is feasible, meets service priorities and complies with NHS quality standards. The NHS will not actively recruit from developing countries in order not to undermine their efforts to provide local healthcare.

5.23   There will be a targeted, nationally co-ordinated campaign using short-term contracts to boost the number of medical consultants and the overall number of doctors in the next three years. There are surpluses of trained doctors in some European countries. We will also recruit from other developed nations, especially in key specialties such as oncology and cardio-thoracic surgery, where expertise is concentrated. Carefully planned and targeted international recruitment for nursing and midwifery also remains part of our strategy.

Conclusion

5.24   The next few years will see a major expansion in staff numbers in the NHS. This expansion has to be sustained. The increases we are making in training numbers will provide for further staff expansion in future years. Getting the most from these new staff – and from existing staff – will, however, require changes in the way people work in the NHS and changes in the way the NHS is run. As the chapters that follow explain, delivering a patient-centred service requires reform as well as investment.

6

Changed systems for the NHS

- New system of devolved responsibility
- Core national standards and targets
- Modernisation Agency to support best practice and improvement
- Independent publication of performance information
- Independent inspection to assure quality
- A new £500 million performance fund
- Intervention in failing health organisation
- Inclusive new ways of running the NHS

Introduction

6.1   This plan outlines a new delivery system for the NHS. It is a system based around the NHS as a 'high trust' organisation. It offers standards and clinical frameworks set nationally. A leaner and more focused centre with the Secretary of State devolving powers. And the chance for health professionals to innovate locally earning greater autonomy the better they perform. With support to spread best practice and pressure to raise consistently poor standards.

6.2   The 1948 settlement assumed central accountability for the NHS. The sound of every dropped bedpan was to reverberate around Whitehall, in Nye Bevan's immortal phrase. But this accountability was more apparent than actual. The reality is that a million patients every day rely on the skills and judgement of highly trained frontline professionals, so the NHS cannot be run from Whitehall.

6.3   The last Government's 'internal market' attempted to address this problem. But by fragmenting the NHS, standards remained variable and best practice was not shared. Competition between hospitals was a weak lever for improvement, because most areas were only served by one or two local general hospitals. Other methods of raising standards were ignored. The market ethos undermined teamwork between professionals and organisations vital to patient-centred care. And it hampered planning across the NHS as a whole, leading to cuts in nurse training and a stalled hospital building programme.

6.4   Our aim is to redesign the system around the patient. That means not repeating the mistakes of the past. The top down government model failed to provide the local innovation, and the responsiveness to deliver sustained improvements in patient care. The internal market imposed a false market on the health service. The result was not better incentives but more fragmentation, a lottery in provision and excess bureaucracy.

A new delivery model

The Plan proposes a new relationship between centre, region and locality.

6.5   It is a model of healthcare that protects and strengthens what is unique about the NHS: the dedication of the staff. The public service ethic that most private companies envy. The NHS is an organisation glued together by a bond of trust between staff and patient or, what some have called, 'principled motivation'. Out aim is to renew that for today's world, not throwing away those values to market mechanisms, but harnessing them to drive up performance. That is why we believe the principles set out at the beginning of this plan, and signed up to by key NHS organisations, are central to the type of NHS we want to create.

6.6   Because we trust people on the frontline, the centre will do only what it needs to do; then there will be maximum devolution of power to local doctors and other health professionals. The principle of subsidiarity will apply. So the centre will: set standards, monitor performance, put in place a proper system of inspection, provide back up to assist modernisation of the service and, where necessary, correct failure. Intervention will be in inverse proportion to success; a system of earned autonomy. The centre will not try and take every last decision. There will be progressively less central control and progressively more devolution as standards improve and modernisation takes hold.

6.7   Moving from the internal market to this new approach has had to be done in stages to ensure that the NHS avoided wholesale disruption. The first stage was set out in the Government's White Paper, the New NHS – published in 1997 – and the Health Act 1999. They gave responsibility for shaping and commissioning care to local groups of doctors and nurses working together. Primary care groups (PCGs) are now up and running in every area and controlling over £20 billion – two thirds of the local NHS budgets. And as from April the first 17 primary care trusts (PCTs) have been in operation giving local health professionals more freedom to develop new services by bringing together in a single organisation primary and community care services. At the same time NHS trusts were maintained but competition was replaced with co-operation. New systems were established to set and monitor national standards. Now we are taking the new model for the NHS a stage further.

6.8   In future the Department of Health's role will involve championing the interests of patients by applying both pressure and support. It will do this by:

- setting the priorities for improving the nation's health, and allocating funding to local health services

- working with patients and the professions to develop national standards of care

- putting in place a robust management and support framework to deliver those standards

- monitoring and holding the NHS to account so that patients know how well the NHS is performing

- intervening on behalf of patients only where NHS organisations are failing to deliver proper standards of care.

Setting priorities and developing standards

6.9   This National Plan sets out the main national priorities. Being clear about the key national priorities creates the space to tackle local priorities.

6.10   Patients should have fair access and high standards of care wherever they live. So at national level the Department of Health will, with the help of leading clinicians, managers and staff, set national standards in the priority areas. These standards will take three forms:

- national standards for key conditions and diseases through National Service Frameworks (NSFs). NSFs have already been produced covering mental health and coronary heart disease and in the autumn will be followed by the country's first ever comprehensive National Cancer Plan. An NSF for older people's services will be published in Autumn 2000 and for diabetes next year. These five service frameworks between them cover around half of total NHS spending. Further NSFs will be developed on a rolling basis over the period of the Plan.

- clear guidance on the best treatments and interventions from the National Institute for Clinical Excellence (NICE). Its work is helping to ensure a faster, more uniform uptake of treatments which work best for patients. This year the National Institute for Clinical Excellence is due to undertake 23 appraisals and to issue 10 sets of guidelines. As part of the NHS Plan we will increase the work programme of the National Institute for Clinical Excellence. It will carry out 50% more appraisals and produce 50% more guidelines. To enable it to carry out this extra work we will increase the National Institute for Clinical Excellence budget by £2 million.

- a limited number of ambitious but achievable national targets. They will include shorter waiting times, the quality of care and facilities for people while they are in hospital, new services to help people remain independent, and efficiency.

Support to redesign care around patients

6.11 Over the past few years the NHS has started to redesign the way health services work – in the outpatient clinic, the casualty department and the GP surgery. The work has been led by staff from across the health service and involves:

- looking at services from the way the patient receives them – asking their views on what is convenient, what works well and what could be improved

- planning the pathway or route that a patient takes from start to finish to see how it could be made easier and swifter – every step, from the moment a patient arrives at the GP up to and including when they are discharged. Unnecessary stages of care are removed, more tests and treatment are done on a one-stop and daycase basis

- best, modern clinical practice is identified, and decisions are made about which professional should best carry out which functions. The result is a standard guideline or protocol for each condition.

6.12 Where this has been done the impact has been dramatic. It has resulted in improved services for patients. It has also resulted in improved productivity, made the task of caring for patients easier for staff and in many cases it has released resources to spend on other services.

In North Tyneside General Hospital, the time the majority of patients spend in accident and emergency has been reduced from three to four hours to 36 minutes on average. This has been achieved by redesigning services for patients not needing to see a doctor when they come into casualty. Specially trained nurses assess patients in accident and emergency and make use of computer-aided decision support to provide the appropriate treatment. The use of nurses in this way enables doctors to concentrate on the patients who require medical treatment.

In West Middlesex University Hospital, services for patients with suspected prostate cancer have been transformed by redesigning the patient's journey. Under the traditional system, patients saw a doctor in an outpatient clinic, returned on more than one occasion for a number of tests, and then again for their results. The hospital team redesigned the process to allow clinical assessment and the tests to be carried out during a single visit, with the results available the following week. The time taken to identify a high risk for prostate cancer fell from six months to a maximum of 18 days.

6.13 Those places blazing the trail for this revolution in patient care demonstrate that the NHS can deliver modern, high quality, convenient services. Spreading best practice in the NHS however is often slow and ad hoc. Too many NHS organisations have been left to sink or swim, without external support to spread service redesign techniques.

Modernisation Agency

6.14 We will now take forward this service redesign approach. Rapid, effective service improvement requires targeted expert support to spread best practice and stimulate change locally. It mirrors the change management approach taken in much of the private sector.

6.15 We will create a new Modernisation Agency to help local clinicians and managers redesign local services around the needs and convenience of patients. It will encompass the existing National Patients' Action Team, the Primary Care Development Team, the 'Collaborative Programmes' and the clinical governance support unit. The NHS Leadership Centre will also become the responsibility of the new Modernisation Agency, as will the Beacon Programme and the NHS annual awards programmes. The Agency will work with all Trusts to support continuous service improvement.

6.16 The Agency's staff will mostly be drawn from the NHS on secondment. The Agency's own regional teams will be based within the Regional Offices, with membership drawn from the NHS and elsewhere. They will work closely with Regional Office staff. Every trust will be expected to set up teams to implement this new patient centred approach in their own organisation. In this way, the Modernisation Agency will enbed a personalised care at the heart of the service.

6.17 In addition to existing work the Agency as its initial work programme will:

- implement three more 'Action On' projects to cut waits and streamline care for orthopaedic, dermatology and ear, nose and throat treatment

- extend the ground-breaking Cancer Collaborative initiative to every cancer service in the country and establish two similar programmes to cut delays for heart treatment and reduce waiting in accident and emergency departments

- more than double the number of primary care groups participating in the improving primary care programme from 40 to over 100

- support a 'healthy communities' collaborative to develop effective ways of improving health particularly in the most deprived areas.

- extend the booked appointment system to every service in every hospital

- lead a major drive in partnership with the National Institute for Clinical Excellence to develop and apply clear national protocols for specific care pathways.

Information on performance standards

6.18   New arrangements for monitoring and reporting the performance of local health services will be established. Already a Performance Assessment Framework (PAF) has been introduced that covers the six key areas of NHS performance: health improvement; fair access to services; effective and appropriate delivery of health care; outcomes from health care; efficient use of resources; high quality experience for patients and carers. Each year tables are published showing how each health authority has performed against the measures in each category.

6.19   As a result of the NHS Plan five changes are being made to the way performance standards are set and information is collected and published:

- the current Performance Assessment Framework primarily applies to health authorities. From next April we will introduce a complementary version of the Performance Assessment Framework that specifically applies to all NHS trusts as well as primary care trusts providing community services. This will enable both Ministers and the public to understand how efficient and effective the providers and deliverers of health services are. This trust-based Performance Assessment Framework will include relevant parts of the health authority Performance Assessment Framework as well as trust specific information on patients' views, quality of care, the workforce, and efficiency

- the current measures of performance in the Performance Assessment Framework are of variable quality. The Department of Health will work with the National Institute for Clinical Excellence, the Commission for Health Improvement, the Audit Commission, patients' organisations and the Royal Colleges to develop proposals for improved measures

- responsibility for the annual publication of the results of the Performance Assessment Framework will be transferred to the Commission for Health Improvement, who will work in association with the Audit Commission. This will demonstrate to the public that the results are independent and genuine. The results will take the form of an annual 'report card' setting out how well each part of the NHS is performing

- information on primary care services needs to be strengthened. By April 2001 every GP practice and primary care group/trust must have in place systems to monitor referral rates from every GP practice, to match the information currently available on GP prescribing

- new efficiency targets will be set. Past NHS efficiency targets have been imposed on the NHS without adequate analysis of what is sensible or achievable locally, and without a proper understanding of their impact on other aspects of care. So in future the new efficiency targets for the NHS will not permit a trade off between cost and quality. And they will be based on levels of service already being achieved by the best trusts around the country. We will use the Performance Assessment Framework to identify those trusts with the best performance for fair access, cost-effectiveness, outcomes of care, and responsiveness to patients. The cost of providing care in these high quality, high performing trusts will become the benchmark for the whole NHS, with all trusts expected to reach the level of the best (green light) trusts over the next 5 years. A new 'best value' regime will require each NHS organisation to review at least one major service, including clinical services, each year.

Inspection

6.20 The NHS, like other public services, needs to be subject to independent scrutiny. Local people have the right to know how effective their local health services are. In addition inspection helps identify all that is good about an organisation as well as highlighting problems that need to be addressed. But until the Government set up the Commission for Health Improvement the NHS lacked any independent inspectorate. Commission for Health Improvement will quality-assure the care of NHS hospitals as well as community and primary care services.

6.21 The Commission for Health Improvement, with the support of the Audit Commission, will inspect every NHS organisation every four years. In addition, organisations rated as 'red' under the Government's system of 'earned autonomy' will be subject to more frequent, two-yearly Commission for Health Improvement inspection. To support this expanded role for the Commission for Health Improvement, its current size is set to double over the next few years.

6.22 The Commission for Health Improvement has just started its rolling programme of inspections. It is expecting to complete 25 inspections this year and a further 100 every year after that. The Commission will discuss with the Medical Royal Colleges how their respective visits programmes can be co-ordinated and possibly integrated.

6.23 The Government will also continue to use its powers to send the Commission into those trusts where there are serious and urgent concerns about clinical practice or patient safety.

6.24 As well as carrying out a series of local inspections the Commission for Health Improvement and the Audit Commission will undertake a complementary series of national studies and inspections.

New incentives and 'earned autonomy'

6.25 Performance improvement in the new NHS will be underpinned from April 2001 by a new system of incentives which will support the delivery of better services for patients. The incentives will offer both financial recognition and non-financial reward to organisations and frontline staff for overall excellence and improved performance.

6.26 Depending on their performance against the Performance Assessment Framework, all NHS organisations (health authorities, NHS trusts, primary care groups, primary care trusts, and health action zones) will for the first time annually and publicly be classified as 'green', 'yellow' or 'red'. Criteria will be set nationally but assessment will be by Regional Offices with independent verification by the Commission for Health Improvement.

6.27 Red organisations will be those who are failing to meet a number of the core national targets. Green organisations will be meeting all core national targets and will score in the top 25% of organisations on the Performance Assessment Framework, taking account of 'value added'. Yellow organisations will be meeting all or most national core targets, but will not be in the top 25% of Performance Assessment Framework performance. So red status will result from poor absolute standards of performance, triggering action (set out below) to ensure a 'floor' level of acceptable performance is achieved throughout the NHS. Green status reflects both outstanding absolute performance against core national targets and relative performance against the wider Performance Assessment Framework measures, serving as an incentive for continuous improvement on the part of all organisations. The 25% threshold for green status will be reviewed periodically.

6.28 Measuring performance across a whole health authority will often mask significant internal variations within it – particularly as health authorities evolve to cover larger populations. So the traffic light status will be accorded to individual NHS organisations. As many aspects of performance span organisations across a health community, the criteria for traffic lights will explicitly include how well they work in partnership with others and how well the local 'health economy' as a whole is performing on key shared objectives.

6.29 The green-light NHS organisations will be rewarded with greater autonomy and national recognition, which within the framework of the local Health Improvement Programme will take the following forms:

- automatic access to the National Performance Fund (see below) and discretionary capital funds without having to bid

- lighter touch monitoring by the Regional Offices

- less frequent monitoring by the Commission for Health Improvement

- greater freedom to decide the local organisation of services

- being used as beacons or exemplars for the Modernisation Agency

- having the ability to take over persistent failure red light organisations.

6.30 In addition, green health authorities will be 'licensed' to take over delegated Regional Office performance management functions in relation to the local NHS including NHS trusts. Over time, within a national framework, this would allow the progressive devolution of performance management and strategic development from the Department of Health, and a streamlining of the 'intermediate' tier.

Financial incentives

6.31 From April 2001 the Government will introduce a National Health Performance Fund building up to £500m a year by 2003/04. The fund, which will be held and distributed regionally, will allow incentives worth on average £5 million for each Health Authority area to be available to reward progress against annually agreed objectives. The intention is to encourage year-on-year improvements regardless of differing local starting points.

6.32 'Green' organisations will have access to their share of the National Performance Fund as of right.

6.33 'Yellow' health authorities, NHS trusts and primary care groups/trusts will be required to agree plans, signed off by the regional office, setting out how they will use their share of the fund to improve their services and contribute to national objectives and local priorities.

6.34 'Red' organisations will have their share of the Performance Fund held by the new Modernisation Agency. They will get their fair share of extra funds but it will come with strings attached. Spending will be overseen by the Modernisation Agency.

6.35 The Performance Fund will include rewards for staff and organisations that reduce waiting times and introduce booked admissions, redesign waiting out of the system and improve the quality of care, including the adoption of local referral protocols based on national clinical guidelines.

6.36 For primary care groups and trusts one of the criteria for access to the funds will be the development and use of incentive schemes that ensure referrals to hospital are appropriate and will help achieve shorter waiting times. Incentives will also be developed for joint working between primary care groups, NHS Trusts and social services to achieve improvements in rehabilitation facilities for older people.

6.37 The Performance Fund will enable NHS trusts and primary care trusts to offer greater incentives to staff in clinical teams and primary health care teams linked to their contribution to service objectives. The reward could take the form of:

- money to buy new equipment or upgrade facilities to improve patient care

- improved facilities and amenities for staff

- non-consolidated cash incentives for individuals and teams.

6.38 As part of these new arrangements we intend to pilot the use of team bonuses in a number of NHS trusts from next year. The results of the pilots will inform our decisions on the further development of team rewards.

Intervention

6.39 Primary care groups and primary care trusts already have the right to begin either providing appropriate services in-house, or to transfer funding and services to alternative providers, where they have serious and persistent concerns about the quality of local hospital services. However this will often be difficult in practice either because of the destabilising consequences for other services within the provider trust (such as the accident and emergency department) or because of the distance that patients would have to travel to alternative providers. By itself, the threat of switching work is, therefore, often a weak lever to drive improvement in a local NHS trust, as was shown by the failures of the internal market.

6.40   For this reason, there need to be new mechanisms directly to intervene to turn round the performance of a seriously failing organisation, in those rare cases where other approaches have not succeeded. Failing organisations will therefore be subject to a rising scale of intervention reflecting the seriousness and persistence of their problems. 'Red' organisations – those whose performance calls for 'special measures' – will receive expert external advice, support and, where necessary, intervention.

6.41   'Red' organisations on special measures will be legally directed to produce a detailed recovery plan, which includes milestones and measures to put right concerns reported by the Commission for Health Improvement. The recovery plan will have to be agreed with, and will be overseen by, regional offices.

6.42   'Red' organisations will receive intensive support from regional offices and the new Modernisation Agency. The share of the National Health Performance Fund that relates to 'red' organisations will be held by the new Modernisation Agency to use for targeted external assistance to help turn around their performance.

6.43   In the case of persistent clinical failure in a 'red light' organisation, NHS trusts will be able to draw on the limited number of medical consultants that the Modernisation Agency will employ on a retainer basis in each region. They will be geographically mobile, and will be seconded in to provide clinical leadership and where appropriate direct patient care in trusts with enduring performance problems.

6.44   As a last resort, those 'red' organisations that exceptionally fail to respond to special measures and meet their recovery plan will be put under the control of a new replacement senior executive, non-executive, and clinical team. Clinicians and managers from 'green' organisations could be deployed for this purpose. Alternatively, expressions of interest could be invited from elsewhere, and subject to a tender from an approved list. Trusts could be merged, or large trusts split up into smaller or different clinical configurations where appropriate.

6.45   Where persistent failure is identified in a primary care group or primary care trust, responsibility for leading primary care in the area affected could be transferred to a neighbouring primary care group or primary care trust on either a temporary or permanent basis.

A new role for Government

6.46   To deliver the new relationships between the Government and the NHS, there will need to be new, more inclusive national and local structures.

6.47   A Modernisation Board will be established to advise the Secretary of State on, and help oversee implementation of the NHS Plan. It will also publish an independent annual report on progress in implementing the NHS Plan. Its membership will include key stakeholders committed to the modernisation of a sustainable tax-funded NHS. They will be health professionals, patient and citizen representatives, and frontline managers drawn from 'green light' NHS organisations.

6.48 Within the Department of Health, the increasingly unhelpful split between public health functions, the NHS, and social services will be overcome by combining responsibility for them in a single chief executive post at permanent secretary level with more autonomy and operational control. The Chief Executive will account to the Modernisation Board for delivery against the Plan.

6.49 Below the Chief Executive and supporting conventional line management arrangements, the Department will establish a small number of Taskforces to drive forward implementation of this Plan. The taskforces are likely to include waiting, heart disease, cancer, mental health, older people, children, inequalities and public health, the workforce, quality, and the capital and information systems infrastructure. Each taskforce will include members from relevant national and local NHS organisations, as well as the national clinical 'czars' and key departmental officials. A member of the Modernisation Board will also serve on each taskforce.

6.50 There will be new written performance agreements between regional offices of the Department and the Chief Executive specifying their contribution to quantifiable deliverables. The Regional Director will be personally accountable for delivery of the agreed performance targets.

6.51 Personal, as well as organisational accountability will be strengthened by giving regional directors a formal role in counter-signing the annual performance reports, personal development plans and performance pay of NHS chief executives.

6.52 National arrangements, modified as appropriate, will be mirrored by regional and local modernisation boards and delivery taskforces. The local Modernisation Boards will be the forum in which local stakeholders, including hospital consultants and patients groups, contribute to the health improvement programme.

6.53 As a consequence of these new arrangements, the Government will devolve and place at arms length powers and responsibilities that do not relate to its core functions. Already responsibility for advising on the take-up and use of drugs and treatments has been placed in the hands of the National Institute for Clinical Excellence. An independent Commission for Health Improvement has been established to inspect every part of the health service. Under the NHS Plan further functions will be devolved from the Secretary of State to other bodies.

6.54 The appointment of non-executive directors of trusts and health authorities will pass to a new arms-length body. For the last decade the power to appoint all 3,000 non-executive directors of NHS trusts and health authorities has rested with the Secretary of State. In future all appointments to these NHS boards will be undertaken by a new NHS Appointments Commission, not Ministers. The Secretary of State will publish guidance for the Appointments Commission on job requirements for non-executives, including support for the core principles of the NHS, and targets for diversity. The Appointments Commission will report annually to Parliament on its performance and progress.

6.55 The Commission will be made up of a chair and eight commissioners, each with a regional role not just in appointing but in on-going support and development of non executives. They will replace the current posts of regional Chairs. Appointments to the Commission will be made on merit by the Secretary of State, following open competition and in strict accordance with Nolan rules.

6.56 Decisions on the outcome of major health service reorganisations will in future be based on the recommendations of an independent panel. The current system, under which the Secretary of State makes decisions on contested proposals, is insensitive, opaque and not sufficiently independent. Too little attention is paid to the impact on the total health care system – including the effect on social services.

6.57 From next year there will be a new National Independent Panel to advise on contested major changes. It will be comprised of around one third doctors, nurses and other health professionals, one third patients' and citizens' representatives, and one third managers of the 'green light' health authorities and trusts in the country. The independent panel will make recommendations to the Secretary of State, assessing proposed changes against clear criteria, including quality of care, community health needs, accessibility, resourcing and the findings of the National Beds Inquiry. It will explicitly take account of the rigour of the local consultation process. The Panel will operate openly, publish its recommendations, the reasons for its conclusions and the evidence it considered.

6.58 The hearing of consultants' appeals against dismissals will in future be dealt with locally rather than by the Secretary of State, bringing the situation in line with normal employment practice.

6.59 The number of directives issued by the Department of Health will be slashed dramatically. Historically up to ten circulars per week are sent to hospitals and primary care organisations. In future that will generally be cut to no more than one shorter communication a week.

Conclusion

6.60 By 2004 there will be a new relationship between the Government and the NHS. Earned autonomy will be working. Devolution will have taken hold.

6.61 To symbolise the new relationship, the Government will ensure that more money goes into frontline services rather than into bureaucracy. Good management is central to delivering patient-centred care. We are already committed, within this first full Parliament, to save £1 billion as a consequence of abolishing the internal market.

6.62 By 2004 the share of NHS spend on management costs will be cut so that a higher share of every pound spent goes into frontline patient care.

6.63 The new model of earned autonomy symbolises the trust that the public and government alike have in frontline NHS staff. But making the new system work to deliver patient-centred care will require changes from those staff too.

7

Changes between health and social services

- one-stop health and social care services
- £900 million investment in new intermediate care services
- new incentive scheme for social services to promote partnership working
- joint Best Value inspections of health and social care organisations
- new Care Trusts to bring health and social services into one organisation

Introduction

7.1 If patients are to receive the best care, then the old divisions between health and social care need to be overcome. The NHS and social services do not always work effectively together as partners in care, so denying patients access to seamless services that are tailored to their particular needs. The division between health and social services can often be a source of confusion for people. Fundamental reforms are needed to tackle these problems.

Developing partnership working

7.2 The Health Act 1999 enables local councils and the NHS to work more closely together. The Act swept away the legal obstacles to joint working by allowing the use of:

- *pooled budgets:* this involves local health and social services putting money into a single dedicated budget to fund a wide range of care services

- *lead commissioning:* either the local authority or the health authority/primary care group takes the lead in commissioning services on behalf of both bodies

- *integrated providers:* local authorities and health authorities merge their services to deliver a one-stop package of care.

7.3 Already Health Act schemes covering budgets of over £200 million are in operation. But only a small minority of patients are benefiting. In future, therefore, we will make it a requirement for these powers to be used in all parts of the country rather than just some. The result will be a new relationship between health and social care. In turn it will bring about a radical redesign of the whole care system. In future, social services will be delivered in new settings, such as GP surgeries, and social care staff will work alongside GPs and other primary and community health teams as part of a single local care network. This co-location of services will make easier the joint assessment of patients' needs. The assessments will form part of the new personal care plan which older patients and others will now receive (see chapter 15).

Somerset Health Authority and Somerset County Council

The two authorities have formed a Joint Commissioning Board which also involves representatives from the voluntary sector and users of services. At the same time staff from health and social services were brought together into one service delivery organisation. The benefit for clients is that they have a single care plan, a single key or link worker and a unified multi-disciplinary team to deal with whatever health or social care need they have.

Intermediate care

7.4 A key test of these closer working arrangements will be how well they provide older people with improved services. In future older people must not be left to find their own way around the system or left in a hospital bed when rehabilitation or supported care is what they need. They must receive the right care at the right time in the right place. This Plan provides an extra £900 million investment by 2003/04 in the new intermediate care and related services to promote independence and improve quality of care for older peaple. With the extra funding for intermediate care, health authorities, primary care groups, primary care trusts and local authorities will have to demonstrate that they will put in place the following services:

- *rapid response teams:* made up of nurses, care workers, social workers, therapists and GPs working to provide emergency care for people at home and helping to prevent unnecessary hospital admissions

- *intensive rehabilitation services:* to help older patients regain their health and independence after a stroke or major surgery. These will normally be situated in hospitals

- *recuperation facilities:* many patients do not always need hospital care but may not be quite fit enough to go home. Short-term care in a nursing home or other special accommodation eases the passage

- *arrangements at GP practice or social work level to ensure that older people receive a one-stop service:* this might involve employing or designating the sort of key workers or link workers used in Somerset or basing case managers in GP surgeries

- *integrated home care teams:* so that people receive the care they need when they are discharged from hospital to help them live independently at home.

7.5   They will have freedom to decide on the precise organisational arrangements for their area.

Joint inspection

7.6   The Commission for Health Improvement, Audit Commission and the Social Services Inspectorate will use the Best Value system jointly to inspect health and social care organisations to see how well they are implementing these arrangements. They will also check on what difference joint working is making in terms of such measures as:

- reducing the number of cases where an older patient's discharge is delayed from hospital

- reducing preventable emergency hospital admission and readmission of older people and those with mental health problems

- the speed at which the needs of older people are assessed.

Incentives for joint working

7.7   Local authorities, health authorities, primary care groups and primary care trusts will receive incentive payments to encourage and reward joint working. In the case of health organisations it will be through the National Performance Fund (see chapter 6). In social services £50 million a year will be available from April 2002 to reward improved social services joint working arrangements based on measuring performance from 2001. From April 2003 the fund will rise to £100 million. It will operate as a ring fenced grant and will be focused initially on intermediate care performance. There will be common criteria between the funds.

Primary care trusts

7.8   Primary care trusts are providing a unique opportunity to foster closer working between health and social services. They have the potential to make real improvements for patients, making the health and social care system easier to understand, simpler to access and more convenient to use. Primary care trusts are already bringing together primary and community health services within a single organisation. By April 2004 we expect all primary care groups to have become primary care trusts. They also provide a suitable means for the commissioning of social care services, using the Health Act flexibilities, for older people and those with mental health problems.

New Care Trusts

7.9   We now propose to establish a new level of primary care trusts which will provide for even closer integration of health and social services. In some parts of the country, health and social services are already working together extremely closely and wish to establish new single multi-purpose legal bodies to commission and be responsible for all local health and social care. The Government intends to build on the establishment of primary care trusts so that all those localities who want to follow this route can do so. This will require changes to the governance arrangements for primary care trusts to ensure representation of health and social care partners. The new body will be known as a 'Care Trust' to reflect its new broader role.

7.10 Care Trusts will be able to commission and deliver primary and community healthcare as well as social care for older people and other client groups. Social services would be delivered under delegated authority from local councils. Care Trusts will usually be established where there is a joint agreement at local level that this model offers the best way to deliver better care services.

7.11 Where local health and social care organisations have failed to establish effective joint partnerships – or where inspection or joint reviews have shown that services are failing – the Government will take powers to establish integrated arrangements through the new Care Trust.

7.12 The establishment of Care Trusts will obviously have to take account of the roll out and capacity of primary care trusts. The first wave of Care Trusts could be in place next year.

Conclusion

7.13 These changes will remove the outdated institutional barriers between health and social services which have got in the way of people getting the care they need when they need it. The new arrangements will provide better care services, especially for older people. These changes in the way organisations work need to be complemented by changes in the way that individual members of NHS staff work.

8

Changes for NHS doctors

- expansion of medical students, specialist registrars, consultants and GPs
- further expansion to follow
- move to new quality-based contracts for GPs
- new arrangements for single-handed practices
- new contract for consultants
- extra rewards for consultants tied to NHS service

Introduction

8.1 Doctors working in primary care and in hospitals work hard for their patients. Both their commitment and skill is highly valued. We have some of the finest doctors in the world. The NHS has to value its doctors by investing more in their skills and their efforts for patients. But the contractual arrangements for GPs and consultants stem from 1948. They are based on arrangements that in important respects are not relevant to today's world. In partnership with doctors and their representatives now is the time to make changes to help deliver the improvements in this Plan.

Family doctors

8.2 Our family doctors are a real source of strength for the NHS. As a result of the changes in this Plan we will have strengthened GP services still further:

- there will be 2,000 more GPs and 450 more GPs in training by 2004. This will just be a start – faster growth of the number of GPs will need to continue beyond 2004

- there will be a bigger role for GPs in shaping local services, as more become specialist GPs, as PCTs become universal and as new care trusts (see chapter 7), incorporating social services as well as health services, come on stream

- pressure on GP services will be eased as nurses and other community staff (see chapter 9) together with a new generation of graduate primary care mental health workers (see chapter 14) take on more tasks

- up to 3,000 family doctors' premises including 500 new primary care centres will benefit from a £1 billion investment programme by 2004

- GPs will be helped with their continuing professional development through earmarked funds

- NHS occupational health services will be extended to cover family doctors.

8.3   The development of primary care services is key to the modernisation of the NHS. However, we need to modernise the relationship between the NHS and GPs, building on what is already good. The current GP contract – the 'red book' – has often worked well, but it gives greater emphasis to the number of patients on a GP's list and the quantity of services provided rather than the quality of them. Too often it has been an obstacle to GPs who have wanted to develop services tailored to the needs of their own local population.

8.4   Family doctors are also looking for better and more flexible ways of working. For example, some GPs want to spend at least part of their career as salaried doctors rather than independent contractors. A significant number want to restructure their practices, perhaps to develop new services by using their staff in new ways or co-operating with other practices in offering care across a local community.

8.5   Since 1998 an increasing number of GPs have been working to a different type of contract – the Personal Medical Services (PMS) contract – instead of working to a standard national contract. Personal Medical Services pays GPs on the basis of meeting set quality standards and the particular needs of their local population. For example, if an area had a particularly high level of heart disease the PMS contract could set targets for ensuring that local people at risk were identified and prescribed appropriate treatment.

8.6   In some Personal Medical Services schemes all members of the healthcare team – doctors, nurses and other health professionals – work on a similar contract instead of the traditional arrangement where staff work for a self-employed GP. Personal Medical Services also allows GPs, if they choose, to work on a salaried part-time or full-time basis.

8.7   This approach has brought a wide range of benefits. It has been used to develop new services for specific populations, such as ethnic minority communities, to attract doctors and nurses into deprived areas and to improve services for patients.

Case study of a PMS scheme in an area of deprivation

Until recently, the Pennywell area of Sunderland could not attract any GP practices to serve a population of approximately 13,500 people. Under PMS, the local NHS trust now employs a GP and fully integrated primary healthcare team to work in partnership with the community and other local agencies. People in this area of high need now have fast access to a wide range of primary care services. These include minor operations, drop in sessions, health promotion, asthma control and breast screening clinics.

Some services require no appointment. In others, appointments take place on the same day of asking and the average wait for an appointment is just one day.

This shift to managed healthcare means a move away from reliance on emergency care. Some 2,300 accident and emergency attendances by patients registered with the Pennywell pilot took place in the year before it went into operation. That number has now fallen by 40%.

8.8 We will encourage a major expansion of Personal Medical Services contracts. All the current pilot schemes that are successful will become permanent. By April 2002 we expect nearly a third of all GPs to be working to Personal Medical Services contracts. And we expect the number to grow steadily over the next four years to form a majority of GPs. Salaried GPs will come to form a growing number of family doctors providing that is what they choose to do. We will make it easier to switch to a Personal Medical Services contract by introducing a standard core contract to help cut bureaucracy. New entrants will, in the future, be able to make a more automatic switch into Personal Medical Services without a lengthy pilot phase. The core contract will ensure basic consistency on delivering key objectives such as access to primary care, national service framework standards, quality and clinical governance.

8.9 As we develop the core Personal Medical Services contract we will work with GPs and their representatives to amend the national 'red book' contract. The revised national contract should reflect the emphasis on quality and improved outcomes inherent in the Personal Medical Services approach. By 2004 both local Personal Medical Services and national arrangements are set to operate within a single contractual framework that will meet the key principles and requirements of a modern NHS. This will be the most significant change to the way GPs work for the NHS since 1948.

Single-handed practices

8.10 It is particularly important to be able to confirm that single-handed practices are offering high standards, because although most single-handed GPs work hard and are committed to their patients, they tend to operate in relative clinical isolation. They do not have the ready support from colleagues enjoyed by GPs in larger practices. The current 'red book' contract is a particularly poor mechanism for protecting quality standards in these practices.

8.11 For this reason, new contractual quality standards will be introduced for single-handed practices. This will either be done through a negotiated change to the 'red book', or if this proves not to be possible, a new national Personal Medical Services contract will be introduced into which all single-handed practices will be transferred by 2004. The role of primary care groups and primary care trusts in promoting and auditing clinical governance will also help reduce isolation and encourage co-operation between GPs.

Hospital doctors

8.12 Hospital doctors do a brilliant job for the NHS. Consultants are specialists whose expertise is highly valued by patients. As a result of the changes in this Plan by 2004 consultants working in the NHS will be benefiting from:

- a major investment in equipment, information technology and facilities described in chapter 4

- a 30% expansion in consultant numbers with further increases in the pipeline as a result of expansion in medical school places and specialist registrar posts. In the first instance this will help end single-handed consultants in hard pressed specialties.

8.13 But we intend to go further. As part of the Government's in principle commitment to major expansion of the consultant grade there will need to be a significant increase in the numbers of specialist registrars. One of the reasons that this has not happened in the past is that local NHS trusts have had to contribute part of the cost of specialist registrar posts. As a result there has been a large gap between the number of specialist registrar posts that have been planned for nationally and the number of posts that have actually been created locally. This will now change. From 2002 the Government will centrally fund all specialist registrar posts provided that agreement can be reached with the medical Royal Colleges and other bodies on curricula and criteria for training recognition.

8.14 In addition, as well as ensuring the creation of specialist registrar posts, the Department of Health will take action to help ensure that the appropriate number of consultant posts are established in NHS trusts across the country. Drawing on national service frameworks, workforce plans will match the new standards of care with the numbers of staff required to implement them. NHS trusts will be performance managed against these standards.

8.15 So there will be a guarantee of more consultants and more future consultants too. There will also be a greater role for consultants in shaping local health services:

- hospital consultants will play a central role in the new local taskforces and modernisation boards that will advise on and oversee the implementation of this NHS Plan in all parts of the country

- strengthened forms of commissioning will draw more directly on the expertise of hospital consultants particularly when it comes to the regional commissioning of specialised tertiary services and in developing long-term service agreements with primary care groups and trusts

- radical new forms of clinically-led care will be piloted. In the first instance, pilots will be established to commission cancer services from the new cancer networks which span a number of individual NHS trusts.

8.16 Over the next decade there will be an unprecedented expansion in the number of consultants working in the NHS. It will be vital to ensure the NHS is getting the maximum contribution possible from both existing and new consultants.

8.17 Expansion on this scale also creates the opportunity to ensure that there is a clear career path for all senior doctors. We have examined two options here. The first would involve expanding the number of non consultant career grade doctors, often on trust specific contracts. This option would allow the NHS to get more fixed clinical sessions from senior doctors without competing with private practice, and it will be kept under review.

8.18 The second option is to make hospital care a consultant delivered service, where there is a clear career structure so that doctors have certainty about how they will progress and where contractual obligations to the NHS are unambiguous. It is this option that both the professions and the Government support in principle. Its implementation, however, will depend upon a new consultants' contract.

8.19 The national consultant contract is largely unchanged since 1948. Most consultants work very hard for the NHS and with tremendous commitment to the NHS. Many are working beyond their contractual commitments. But the way consultants are managed on the ground through their current contract is far from satisfactory. For instance, too few have proper job plans setting out their key objectives, tasks and responsibilities and when they are expected to carry out these duties. Even fewer have their performance regularly reviewed. The issue of consultants' private practice has remained a legacy of the 1948 settlement.

8.20 Consultants who make the biggest commitment to the NHS do not get the right rewards. In consultation with doctors and their representatives, we will, therefore, fundamentally overhaul the contract to reward and incentivise those who do most for the NHS.

8.21 As we have already agreed in principle with the British Medical Association, the new contract will make annual appraisal and effective job plans mandatory for all consultants. This process will enable the professional and clinical needs of consultants to be identified and support clinical governance and revalidation. It must also ensure that NHS employers are able to manage the consultant workforce effectively in order to ensure the best use of their time and of the resources of the trust. Royal Colleges will be able to advise NHS trusts on, but not veto, the content of job descriptions for consultant posts. All consultants will have job plans specified by the employer linked to annual appraisal of their work.

8.22 Consideration has been given to 'buying out' the bulk of existing private practice nationally. However, careful analysis suggests this would be unlikely to work in practice: it would probably cost at least £700 million; the NHS would have to enter a bidding war with the private sector; it would seriously distort incentives; and it would be insensitive to local requirements. A different approach will therefore be taken.

8.23 At present, the consultants' contract requires them to work an ambiguous 'five to seven' fixed sessions a week. In future, existing consultants will, by default, be required contractually to undertake seven fixed sessions a week pro rata. Trusts will be able to fund extra, fixed consultant sessions on an as-needed basis, as at present. Assuming this condition and other aspects of the reformed consultant contract are being met, existing consultants will continue to be able to undertake private practice in their own time.

8.24 A move to a consultant-delivered service means that in future, newly qualified consultants will be contracted to work exclusively for the NHS for perhaps the first seven years of their career, providing eight fixed sessions, and more of the service delivery out of hours. In return we plan to increase the financial rewards to newly qualified consultants. Beyond this, the right to undertake private practice will depend on fulfilling job plan and NHS service requirements, including satisfactory appraisals. If agreement cannot be secured to these changes the Government will look to introduce a new specialist grade for newly qualified hospital specialists to secure similar objectives.

8.25 Over time we want to make clearer the advantages of making a long-term commitment to the NHS, particularly for those who will become consultants in the future. First, doctors – as well as nurses and other staff – who are working hardest for the NHS and improving services for patients, will have access to bonus payments from the National Performance Fund. Second, we will reform the existing distinction awards and discretionary points schemes. Together they provided £170 million last year in superannuable bonus payments – ranging from £2,500 to £60,460 – to consultants. But they are not sufficiently related to the NHS work these doctors undertake. They will be merged into a single, more graduated scheme with increased funding: to enable more awards to be made; to ensure that the bulk of any new awards go to consultants who are making the biggest contribution to delivery and improving local health services; and to ensure that bigger rewards go to consultants who make a long-term commitment to the NHS:

- following consultation with doctors and their representatives, we will publish explicit new criteria for the new single scheme by the end of the year. The new arrangements will come into force by April 2001

- by 2004 we will aim to increase the number of consultants in receipt of a superannuable bonus from under one half of all consultants at present to around two-thirds and to double the proportion of consultants who receive annual bonuses of £5,000 or more

- the new scheme will be weighted so that consultants who are contracted exclusively to the NHS have accelerated access to proportionately bigger bonuses

- there will still be special provision for clinical academics (and for the first time academic GPs) and those consultants of national and international renown.

8.26 The new consultant contract will make clear that in the early and middle part of their careers, consultants will be expected to devote the bulk of their time to direct clinical care. It will also stipulate, however, that towards the end of their careers, consultants will have the flexibility to reduce their fixed clinical sessions without detriment to their pensions. We envisage a greater role for mentoring, training and leadership, for example.

Medical education

8.27 We will modernise the Senior House Officer grade, with the aim of providing better and broader educational experience and a reduction in inappropriate workload. New arrangements will be introduced progressively from September 2001. Junior doctors' hours will continue to fall.

8.28 We will rationalise the complex arrangement for medical education. As a first step we will establish a new body – the Medical Education Standards Board – to provide a coherent, robust and accountable approach to postgraduate medical education, replacing the separate bodies for general practice (the Joint Committee for Postgraduate Training in General Practice) and hospital specialties (the Specialist Training Authority). The Board will ensure that patient interests and the service needs of the NHS are fully aligned with the development of the curriculum and approval of training programmes. Membership of the new body will be drawn from the medical profession, the NHS and the public. It will accredit NHS organisations as training providers. We will wish to see consideration of options for overseeing medical undergraduate curricula considered as part of the radical review of the role of the General Medical Council, together with proposals for shortening the medical undergraduate course to three years for existing graduates and four years for others.

Clinical governance

8.29 The overwhelming majority of doctors provide safe, high quality care for patients. Medicine, however, is not an exact science. Mistakes do and will sometimes happen. The NHS has a responsibility to ensure that it has the right systems in place to keep mistakes to a minimum and to learn from them when they happen. That is why the Government has put a new focus on improving service quality. Patients have the right to expect assurances about the quality of care that they receive wherever they receive it in the NHS. There are new national standards, new systems of quality improvement and, for the first time, a statutory duty of quality on all NHS organisations. The new system of clinical governance is being introduced into all parts of the NHS. There will be extra targeted investment in doctors continuing professional development to ensure that all doctors can meet the highest quality standards and requirements of clinical governance and revalidation, coupled with new regulatory safeguards (see chapter 10).

Conclusion

8.30 The health service has much to be proud of in terms of the quality and reputation of its doctors. By 2004 there will be more doctors in the NHS with better rewards. They will be working in new ways to new contracts. Their ability to deliver redesigned services for patients, however, is partly dependent on developing new roles for nurses and other NHS staff.

9

Changes for nurses, midwives, therapists and other NHS staff

- new skills and new roles for nurses
- £140 million extra by 2003/04 for staff to develop their own skills
- Individual Learning Accounts for all support staff
- modernised education and training with a core curriculum
- 'modern matrons' with authority on the wards
- 1,000 nurse consultants and a new grade of consultant therapists
- NHS Leadership Centre and dedicated service modernisation sessions

Introduction

9.1   NHS staff, at every level, are the key to reform. Extra staff will bring big benefits. But expanding the size of the workforce will not on its own be sufficient to deliver the major improvements in patient services the country needs. Radical changes are needed in the way staff work to reduce waiting times and deliver modern, patient-centred services. This is not a question of staff working harder. It is about working smarter to make maximum use of the talents of all the NHS workforce. The changes described in this chapter will offer better services for patients and more opportunities for staff.

Breaking down barriers between staff

9.2   Throughout the NHS the old hierarchical ways of working are giving way to more flexible team working between different clinical professionals. Midwives, for example, are leading more responsive childbirth services in many parts of the country. In many accident and emergency departments nurses are treating patients with minor injuries and ailments, freeing up doctors' time and so delivering shorter waits for treatment. In some community clinics teams made up of occupational therapists, district nurses, physiotherapists and social care staff, working flexibly together across traditional boundaries have halved the length of stay for orthopaedic patients and enabled more frail people to stay at home.

9.3   For every example of good practice there are too many examples where change has yet to take place. Best practice can no longer be an option. Managers and clinicians across the NHS must make change happen.

Modern acute care

At the Central Middlesex Hospital in west London a willingness by all clinical staff to challenge traditional professional boundaries has led to new practices across the hospital:

- in accident and emergency services, extending nursing and radiographer roles has allowed the creation of two community based nurse led accident services connected to the hospital through a telemedicine link

- in critical care, nurse practitioners support patients with coronary care, intensive care and high dependency needs

- in the new Ambulatory Care and Diagnostic Centre, therapists have extended roles and nurses work across the whole patient pathway providing ambulatory patients with real continuity of care from admission to discharge.

9.4 By 2004 the majority of NHS staff will be working under agreed protocols identifying how common conditions should be handled and which staff can best handle them. The new NHS Modernisation Agency will lead a major drive to ensure that protocol based care takes hold throughout the NHS. It will work with the National Institute for Clinical Excellence, patients, clinicians and managers to develop clear protocols that make the best use of all the talents of NHS staff and which are flexible enough to take account of patients' individual needs.

9.5 The new approach will shatter the old demarcations which have held back staff and slowed down care. NHS employers will be required to empower appropriately qualified nurses, midwives and therapists to undertake a wider range of clinical tasks including the right to make and receive referrals, admit and discharge patients, order investigations and diagnostic tests, run clinics and prescribe drugs, as descibed below.

Chief Nursing Officer's 10 key roles for nurses

- to order diagnostic investigations such as pathology tests and X-rays

- to make and receive referrals direct, say, to a therapist or a pain consultant

- to admit and discharge patients for specified conditions and within agreed protocols

- to manage patient caseloads, say for diabetes or rheumatology

- to run clinics, say, for ophthalmology or dermatology

- to prescribe medicines and treatments

- to carry out a wide range of resuscitation procedures including defibrillation

- to perform minor surgery and outpatient procedures

- to triage patients using the latest IT to the most appropriate health professional

- to take a lead in the way local health services are organised and in the way that they are run.

9.6   As part of this approach by 2001, around 23,000 nurses will have the right to prescribe a limited range of medicines. We will then extend both the range of medicines which can be prescribed and the numbers of nurses who can do so. The introduction this year of 'Patient Group Directions', which enable nurses and other professionals to supply medicines to patients according to protocols authorised by a doctor and a pharmacist, will mean that by 2004 a majority of nurses should be able to prescribe.

9.7   Midwives too will develop their role in public health and family well-being. They will work with local doctors and nurses in developing maternity and child health services and Sure Start projects.

9.8   Pharmacists will be able to take on a new role as they shift away from being paid mainly for the dispensing of individual prescriptions towards rewarding overall service. Proposals will be invited for Personal Medical Services-type schemes, that pilot alternative contracts for community pharmacy services. They will cover areas such as medicines management and repeat prescribing.

9.9   Other key groups of staff including therapists, scientists and health visitors will develop their professional roles. Local clinical teams will need to review the care being delivered, how and by whom.

9.10   The Commission for Health Improvement will monitor performance in each NHS organisation to ensure that the new powers are genuinely available to clinical staff who are competent and confident enough to take them on.

Training and development for staff

9.11   To help people to take on these new roles there will be an extra £140 million by 2003/04 to support a major programme of training and development for all staff.

9.12   For professional staff there will be investment to support their continuing development. All members of staff should receive support from their employers to fulfil the requirements of clinical governance and revalidation. We will enter immediate discussions with the professions and NHS employers about how to ensure this commitment is guaranteed. We will review existing requirements for re-registration in nursing. Better use will be made of the investment in continuing professional development with greater emphasis on accredited workplace based systems of learning.

9.13 The NHS has neglected for too long the need to invest in the skills and potential of staff who do not have a professional qualification. That will now change. Over the next three years we will guarantee all such staff access either to an Individual Learning Account of £150 a year or dedicated training to NVQ level two and three. This investment will help the NHS make better use of the potential of healthcare assistants, operating department practitioners, pharmacy technicians and others. New national occupational standards will be developed for this group of workers. These staff will play a key part in raising standards in the fundamentals of patient care. Proposals will be published for the effective regulation of health support workers.

9.14 Staff will also be given the necessary training to take on new roles altogether. We propose to create assistant practitioners in radiography, appropriately trained and qualified, to take mammograms under the supervision of a radiographer. This will release radiographers to extend their role into some of the tasks traditionally undertaken by radiologists, thereby significantly increasing capacity for our breast-screening programme. (see paragraph 14.5)

9.15 This principle can be extended to other areas of care, building on Royal College proposals for a physician's assistant. We will identify the scope for similar action, particularly in some specialties where waiting times are longest and workforce shortages greatest. A timetable for action will be published later this year.

Modernising education and training

9.16 Radical reform is required in NHS education and training to reshape care around the patient.

9.17 The new model of nurse education and training, described in our nursing, midwifery and health visiting strategy, *Making a Difference,* with its emphasis on improving access, developing practical skills earlier in training and with stepping off points at the end of the first year will be rolled out nationwide. By autumn 2001, 85% of all nurse training organisations will be operating the new arrangements. By autumn 2002 it will be standard across the whole of England. Similar principles will be applied to education and training for the other health professions and health scientists.

9.18 There will be reforms to the health curricula to give everyone working in the NHS the skills and knowledge to respond effectively to the individual needs of patients. There will be new joint training across professions in communication skills and in NHS principles and organisation. They will form part of a new core curriculum for all education programmes for NHS staff. By 2002, it will be a pre-condition of qualification to deliver patient care in the NHS that an individual has demonstrated competence in communication with patients. A new common foundation programme will be put in place to enable students and staff to switch careers and training paths more easily. Nurses, midwives or therapists who want to become doctors, for example, will no longer have to start their training from scratch. We will be looking for innovation of this kind in allocating the next tranche of medical school places.

9.19 The NHS is also committed to building a diverse workforce and using its leverage as an employer to make a difference to the life opportunities and health of its local community. Education programmes must open up opportunities in healthcare to the whole of the local community.

Leadership

9.20 Delivering the Plan's radical change programme will require first class leaders at all levels of the NHS.

9.21 Action needs to start in hospitals. The public consultation provoked a strong call for a 'modern matron' figure – a strong clinical leader with clear authority at ward level – and we will do it. The ward sister or charge nurse will be given authority to resolve clinical issues, such as discharge delays and environmental problems such as poor cleanliness. By April 2002 every hospital will have senior sisters and charge nurses who are easily identifiable to patients and who will be accountable for a group of wards. They will be in control of the necessary resources to sort out the fundamentals of care, backed up by appropriate administrative support. In this way patients' demand for a 'modern matron' will be met.

9.22 There will be other new clinical leaders. By 2004 there will be around 1,000 nurse consultants employed in the NHS. By then a first generation of therapist consultant will have started work. They will work with senior hospital doctors, nurses and midwives in drawing up local clinical and referral protocols alongside primary care colleagues.

9.23 We need clinical and managerial leaders throughout the health service. The best NHS leaders are outstanding. There are simply too few of them. NHS organisations should be led by the brightest and the best of public sector management. Leadership development in the NHS has always been ad hoc and incoherent with too few clinicians in leadership roles and too little opportunity for board members to develop leadership skills. That will now change.

9.24 Service modernisation relies on staff – especially those in clinical posts – having the time and space to redesign and re-organise their services. That is what staff throughout the NHS want to do. Relentless daily service pressures often make that difficult. We will introduce 'service modernisation sessions' throughout the NHS where local managers and clinicians can apply the lessons that have been learned elsewhere in the NHS to redesign local services. They will be helped by the NHS Modernisation Agency.

9.25 We will provide management support and training for clinical and medical directors to better equip them for their leadership tasks. Local trusts will be expected to open these posts to competition.

9.26 To deliver a step change in the calibre of NHS leadership, the Government will establish a new Leadership Centre for Health. Operating through the NHS Modernisation Agency the Leadership Centre will be in place by 2001. The Centre will promote leadership development closely tied to the Modernisation Agency's work to deliver improved patient services. It will benefit all staff by widening access to work based development programmes, delivered online as well as face to face. It will provide tailored support for clinicians and managers with leadership potential at different stages in their careers and for those already in leadership roles. Its target group will include people who run service departments, clinical services and community based networks who want to stay in the front line as well as those who seek to progress into executive roles. Chair and non-executive development will form part of its remit. It will be open to social care organisations.

Conclusion

9.27 Developing the skills and potential of NHS staff is a fundamental part of this Plan. The Government is committed to giving them the support they need in order to make the most of their contribution to patient-centred care. By liberating the potential of staff the NHS can shape its services around the needs of patients.

10

Changes for patients

- more information for patients
- greater patient choice
- patient advocates and advisers in every hospital
- redress over cancelled operations
- patients' forums and citizens' panels in every area
- new national panel to advise on major reorganisations of hospitals
- stronger regulation of professional standards

Introduction

10.1 Patients are the most important people in the health service. It doesn't always appear that way. Too many patients feel talked at, rather than listened to. This has to change. NHS care has to be shaped around the convenience and concerns of patients. To bring this about, patients must have more say in their own treatment and more influence over the way the NHS works. The reforms outlined here give patients new rights and new roles within the health service.

Information to empower patients

10.2 Patients will have far greater information about how they can look after their own health and about their local health services. The "Expert Patient" Programme will be extended. The National Institute for Clinical Excellence will publish patient-friendly versions of all its clinical guidelines. Patients will be helped to navigate the maze of health information through the development of NHS Direct online, Digital TV and NHS Direct information points in key public places. This will include information on local NHS dentistry.

10.3 Patients will for the first time also have the option of having much greater information about the treatment that is being planned for them. Patients have the right to see their medical records, though in practice much communication between professionals is not available to the patient concerned. Patients often do not know why they are being referred, or what is being said about them. In future, as a result of this NHS Plan:

- letters between clinicians about an individual patient's care will be copied to the patient as of right

  - smart cards for patients, allowing easier access to health records, will be introduced when the necessary infrastructure has been put in place and we have fully evaluated technical feasibility and effectiveness.

10.4 These innovations will give the patient a clear explanation of what is happening to them and why. They will provide the patient with a personal record of their contact with the health service.

Strengthening patient choice

10.5 Patient choice will be strengthened. Patients have the right to choose a GP. To make it easier for patients to exercise informed choice, a much wider range of information will be published about each GP practice including: list size; accessibility; and performance against standards in national service frameworks. Figures will also be published on the number of patients each practice removes from their list.

10.6 Patients' choice over hospital treatment will be improved by ensuring that by 2005, every patient will be able to book every hospital appointment and elective admission giving them a choice of a convenient date and time rather than being assigned a time by the hospital.

10.7 The choice GPs are able to exercise on behalf of their patients is also important. Prior to 1991, GPs could refer patients to the hospital of their choice. The introduction of the NHS internal market changed that because GPs who were not 'fundholders' could no longer automatically refer patients outside their local area. Instead the patients' and GPs' choice was second-guessed by the health authority who could withhold approval for an 'extra contractual referral'. Since 1999 the creation of primary care groups and trusts has restored choice of referrals to GPs. GPs collectively now decide where to fund services. Ninety-two per cent of patients say they are given appropriate choice about where their GP refers them for hospital treatment. But in those cases where this does not happen primary care groups will be able to act on published information about patients' views of hospital services by moving service agreements from one hospital to another.

Protection for patients

10.8 Standards of care for patients are often good in the NHS. Sometimes, however, they need to be better. New quality assurance systems are already being introduced in the NHS to raise standards. Now this NHS Plan will introduce new mechanisms to satisfy patients that the care they get is quality assured.

10.9 We will establish a full mandatory reporting scheme for adverse healthcare events. There will be a full single database for analysing and sharing the lessons from incidents and near misses in place from the end of 2001, with the framework in place by the end of this year. This will help clinicians to minimise the risk to their patient and improve the quality and safety of patient care.

10.10 The NHS will also have new rapid and robust mechanisms for dealing with under and poor performance among individual doctors. Following extensive consultation, the Department of Health will now implement the Chief Medical Officer's proposals in *Supporting Doctors, Protecting Patients*. All doctors employed in or under contract to the NHS will, as a condition of contract, be required to participate in annual appraisal, and clinical audit, from 2001. This will underpin, and provide much of the data to support, the General Medical Council's mandatory five-yearly revalidation process, which is likely to begin in 2002. Subject to Parliament, by April 2001 all doctors working in primary care, whether principals, non-principals or locums, will be required to be on the list of a health authority and be subject to clinical governance arrangements. These will include annual appraisal and mandatory participation in clinical audit.

10.11 A National Clinical Assessment Authority will be established as an arms-length Special Health Authority from April 2001. Its board will be appointed under Nolan principles. Where concern has arisen locally, it will provide a rapid and objective expert assessment of an individual doctor's performance, recommending to the health authority or employing trust educational or other approaches as appropriate. It will mean an end to the current arrangement where doctors can remain suspended for years while concerns or allegations about their practice are resolved.

10.12 The NHS Tribunal will be abolished, and the power to suspend or remove GPs from a health authority's list will be devolved to health authorities, subject to a right of appeal to the Family Health Services Appeals Authority, from 2001. The right of consultants to appeal against disciplinary action direct to the Secretary of State under the 'paragraph 190' arrangements will end, so that responsibility is devolved from the Secretary of State to NHS trusts locally, from 2001.

10.13 The regulation of the clinical professions and individual clinicians also needs to be strengthened. As a minimum, the self regulatory bodies must change so that they:

- are smaller, with much greater patient and public representation in their membership

- have faster more transparent procedures, and

- develop meaningful accountability to the public and the health service.

10.14 Our proposals for new regulatory bodies for nursing, midwifery and health visiting and for professions allied to medicine, on which we will be consulting shortly, meet these tests. They are the minimum tests that must be met by a reformed General Medical Council. But the GMC should also explore introducing a civil burden of proof and making other reforms if it is to genuinely protect patients. Government and Parliament will have to judge whether the reforms proposed by the GMC following its own consultation process will indeed protect patients and restore public and professional confidence.

10.15 There also needs to be formal co-ordination between the health regulatory bodies. For this reason, a UK Council of Health Regulators will be established, including the GMC, the successor bodies to the UKCC for Nursing Midwifery and Health Visiting, and the Council for Professions Supplementary to Medicine, as well as the General Dental Council, the General Optical Council, the Royal Pharmaceutical Society, the General Osteopaths Council and the General Chiropractic Council. In the first instance the new body would help co-ordinate and act as a forum in which common approaches across the professions could be developed for dealing with matters such as complaints against practitioners. Were concerns to remain about the individual self-regulatory bodies, its role could evolve.

10.16 These modernised and more accountable professional regulatory arrangements will work alongside the NHS's own quality assurance arrangements to offer better protection for patients.

A new patient advocacy service

10.17 When patients are concerned that the NHS is not delivering for them they should get their concerns addressed. As a result of this plan:

- by 2002, an NHS-wide Patient Advocacy and Liaison Service (PALS) will be established in every trust, beginning with every major hospital, with an annual national budget of around £10 million.

10.18 Patients need an identifiable person they can turn to if they have a problem or need information while they are using hospital and other NHS services. Usually situated in the main reception areas of hospitals the new patient advocate team will act as a welcoming point for patients and carers and a clearly identifiable information point. Patient advocates will act as an independent facilitator to handle patient and family concerns, with direct access to the chief executive and the power to negotiate immediate solutions. In mental health and learning disability services, the Patient Advocate and Liaison Service team will build on and support current specialist advocacy services.

10.19 Patient advocates will be able to steer patients and families towards the complaints process where necessary. The Patient Advocacy and Liaison Services will take on the roles which community health councils currently fulfil, of supporting complainants. We will work with other organisations, such as Citizens Advice Bureaux, to ensure additional support for people complaining.

A similar service is already running in Brighton. Since 1994, patient contacts have increased from 98 to over 1000. Anecdotally, 28% of contacts start as an intended formal complaint, but after advice is given and any on-the-spot remedial action is taken with staff concerned, this is reduced to 5%. The Brighton work has also resulted in changes to induction training, care delivery, facilities, décor, and process to deal with sensitive issues such as bereavement.

Rights of redress

10.20 Patients will have the right to redress when things go wrong. They need to know that problems will be sorted out and put right. As a result of this NHS Plan:

- from 2002, when a patient's operation is cancelled by the hospital on the day of surgery for non-clinical reasons, the hospital will have to offer another binding date within a maximum of the next 28 days or fund the patient's treatment at the time and hospital of the patient's choice.

10.21 Patients have the right to complain. Complaints are not always dealt with quickly, with resolution often taking months. The role of the independent convenor has been criticised and the overall complaints procedure is not seen as being independent or transparent. The NHS needs to find a better way of dealing with patients' concerns, preferably before they become official complaints. The NHS also needs to be seen to say sorry where things go wrong, rather than taking a defensive attitude, and to learn from complaints so that the same problems do not recur. The Government is at present evaluating the complaints procedure, taking evidence from a wide range of sources. The Government will act on the outcome of this evaluation and reform the complaints procedure to make it more independent and responsive to patients. Making the complaints procedure less adversarial should result in fewer clinical negligence claims against the NHS. We will look to make further changes to the current system of clinical negligence.

10.22 By 2001 a new NHS Charter will replace the current Patients Charter. It will make clear how people can access NHS services, what the NHS commitment is to patients, and the rights and responsibilities patients have within the NHS.

Consent

Following criticism that patients may not be properly involved in decisions about resuscitation, we are acting to ensure that by next April every hospital will have implemented a local resuscitation policy based on guidelines published by the British Medical Association and Royal College of Nursing.

A series of recent incidents has raised serious concerns about the process by which patients and relatives give informed consent. We are, therefore, also working on how best to ensure good consent practice. We need to change the culture to recognise the central importance of the rights of each patient. Working with clinicians and academics throughout the NHS – in both clinical and research settings, we will involve patients and their representatives fully in this review, so that the changes we make have the confidence of all those who use the NHS. These changes will be introduced from next year.

Patients' views

10.23 In 1974, the then Government tried to give greater prominence to the views of patients by creating community health councils. They attempted to combine three distinct functions: supporting individual patients and complainants; monitoring local hospital and community (but not primary care) services; and providing a citizen's perspective on service changes. It is time to modernise, deepen and broaden the way that patient views are represented within the NHS. As a result of this NHS Plan:

- all NHS trusts, primary care groups and primary care trusts will have to ask patients and carers for their views on the services they have received

- all patients leaving hospital will be given the opportunity to record their views about the standards of care they have received in writing or electronically through new bedside TV information services.

- every local NHS organisation, as well as care homes, will be required to publish, in a new Patient Prospectus, an annual account of the views received from patients – and the action taken as a result. The Patient Prospectus will set out the range of local services available, the ratings they have received from patients and the place they occupy under the Performance Assessment Framework.

10.24 For the first time financial rewards for trusts will be linked to the results of the annual National Patients Survey, a methodologically robust measure of patients views about local NHS services (see paragraph 6.25).

- a Patients' Forum will be established in every NHS trust and primary care trust to provide direct input from patients into how local NHS services are run. For the first time patients will have direct representation on every NHS trust board – elected by the Patients' Forum. The Patients' Forum will have half of its members drawn from local patients groups and voluntary organisations. The other half of the Forum's members will be randomly drawn from respondents to the trust's annual patient survey. The Forum will be supported by the new Patient Advocate and Liaison Service, and will have the right to visit and inspect any aspect of the trust's care at any time. Patient Advocate and Liaison Service staff and forum members will have access to the new NHS Leadership Centre's programmes.

Scrutiny of the NHS

10.25 Local authorities are an important democratically-elected tier of government. As they modernise they will become more effective channels for the views of local people.

10.26 As a result of this Plan local government will be given the power to scrutinise the NHS locally. Chief executives of NHS organisations will be required to attend the main local authority scrutiny all-party committee at least twice annually if requested.

10.27 The power to refer major planned changes in local NHS services to the Secretary of State will transfer from unelected community health councils to the all-party scrutiny committees of elected local authorities. The council scrutiny committees – which must meet in public – will be able to refer contested major service reconfigurations to the new Independent Reconfiguration Panel (see paragraph 6.50). Clear criteria will be set out on the definition of a major service change that can appropriately be referred for consideration nationally.

Patients represented throughout the NHS

10.28 Patients and citizens have had too little influence at every level of the NHS. As a result of this Plan, each health authority area will be required to establish an independent local advisory forum chosen from residents of the area, to provide a sounding board for determining health priorities and policies, including the Health Improvement Programme.

10.29 There will be major increases in the citizen and lay membership of all the professional regulatory bodies, including the General Medical Council.

10.30 One third of the members of the new NHS Modernisation Board will be citizen and patient representatives.

10.31 Citizens and patient representatives will make up one third of the new Independent Reconfiguration Panel on contested major service changes.

10.32 The Commission for Health Improvement will include citizen and lay inspectors on all its review teams.

10.33 Older people will be represented on Commission for Health Improvement inspection teams to ensure older people's dignity and interests are fully taken into account in all inspections.

10.34 A new Citizens Council will be established to advise the National Institute for Clinical Excellence on its clinical assessments. It will complement the work of the NICE Partners Council which provides a forum for the health service and industry to comment on the work of NICE.

Conclusion

10.35 These are far reaching and fundamental reforms which will bring patients and citizens into decision-making at every level. They represent a significant change from 1948. There will be changes to existing structures for representing patients and entirely new ones. A tier of elected government in England other than in Whitehall will be involved in scrutinising the local NHS. This is a package of radical reform. It will enhance and encourage the involvement of citizens in redesigning the health service from the patient's point of view. As a result community health councils will be abolished and funding redirected to help fund the new Patient Advocate and Liaison Service and the other new citizens empowerment mechanisms set out above.

11

Changes in the relationship between the NHS and the private sector

- concordat between the NHS and private providers
- public-private partnerships to modernise NHS services
- expansion of clinical trials for new drugs
- NHSplus to offer occupational health services for employers

Introduction

11.1   The NHS is a huge organisation. Using extra capacity and extra investment from voluntary and private sector providers can benefit NHS patients. The Private Finance Initiative is already delivering new hospitals, on time, to budget as part of the biggest hospital building programme in the history of the NHS. The NHS already spends over £1 billion each year on buying care and specialist services from hospitals, nursing homes and hospices run by private companies and charities. The time has now come for the NHS to engage more constructively with the private sector, and at the same time make more of its own expertise available to employers throughout the country.

The basis for a new relationship

11.2   For decades there has been a stand-off between the NHS and the private sector providers of healthcare. This has to end. Ideological boundaries or institutional barriers should not stand in the way of better care for NHS patients. Public funding for the NHS will increase substantially over the next four years. The private and voluntary sectors have a role to play in ensuring that NHS patients get the full benefit from this extra investment. By constructing the right partnerships the NHS can harness the capacity of private and voluntary providers to treat more NHS patients.

11.3   Developing these new forms of partnership will not compromise the fundamental principles underpinning this Plan: that healthcare should be available on the basis of need, not ability to pay. There is a world of difference between the NHS paying to have patients treated, as NHS patients, in a private hospital for free, and what some propose – forcing patients out of the NHS to pay for their own care. Under our proposals a patient would remain an NHS patient even if they were being treated in the private sector. NHS care will remain free at the point of delivery, whether care is provided by an NHS hospital, a local GP, a private sector hospital or by a voluntary organisation.

11.4   High standards of care for patients and good value for money for taxpayers will have to underpin any arrangements between the two sectors.

A new concordat

11.5   In many areas NHS services are already delivered in close partnership with the private sector. The problem is that most of the arrangements are ad hoc and short term. This way of working provides a poor basis for partnership and value for money.

11.6   As part of the NHS Plan for the first time there will be a national framework for partnership between the private and voluntary sector and the NHS. It will include a set of national guidelines to help primary care groups and trusts when they commission services.

11.7   These new arrangements will be set out in a concordat between the NHS and the private sector covering private and voluntary providers. The concordat will highlight three particular areas for co-operative working:

- *elective care:* this could take the form of NHS doctors and nurses using the operating theatres and facilities in private hospitals or it could mean the NHS buying certain services

- *critical care:* this will provide for the NHS and the private sector to be able to transfer patients to and from each other whenever clinically appropriate

- *intermediate care:* this will involve the private and voluntary sector developing and making available facilities to support the Government's strategy for better preventive and rehabilitation services.

11.8   Clear cost arrangements, particularly when patients are transferred as emergency cases, will need to be established before the concordat takes effect locally.

11.9   Having these facilities available will help the NHS with winter planning and the drive to reduce waiting times. The concordat will also cover:

- the involvement of private and voluntary sector organisations in the development of local health planning

- the development of locally agreed protocols for referral, admission and discharge into and out of NHS and private and voluntary sector facilities

- greater exchange of information between the two sectors about workforce and other capacity issues, and about clinical activity.

11.10 The concordat is intended to be the start not the end of a more constructive relationship. The NHS will explore with the private sector the potential for investment in services – such as pathology and imaging and dialysis. The Government is investing in improvements in these services and wants to help the NHS make the fastest progress possible. Already a number of NHS trusts share or lease facilities. We will encourage more arrangements of this kind by negotiating national call-off contracts with a number of major suppliers. We also propose to develop some partnership arrangements at a regional level for modernising pathology services.

The pharmaceutical and bio-pharmaceutical industries

11.11 The pharmaceutical industry is a UK success story, employing over 60,000 skilled workers and maintaining an annual trade surplus of over £2 billion. The industry is also the UK's leading investor in research and development. The NHS has a major role to play in ensuring that the UK remains an attractive base for the industry. Earlier this year the Pharmaceutical Industry Competitiveness Task Force was established to help develop a deeper partnership between industry, the NHS and Government. Already the task force has agreed that pharmaceutical industry involvement in the development and implementation of national service frameworks would benefit both the NHS and industry.

11.12 Research and development is the key to the future flow of new medicines for the benefit of patients and is the cornerstone of a successful pharmaceutical industry. We must ensure that there are no unnecessary delays in conducting research whilst still protecting the interests of patients. A new policy on research governance in the NHS will be published by the end of the year. By April 2001 we will have developed ways of streamlining the work of research ethics committees whilst preserving all the necessary safeguards. This will allow faster and more effective recruitment of patients into clinical trials, enabling new medicines to be brought on stream more quickly. In addition the new NHS cancer research network will be evaluated as a model for enhancing recruitment into and management of trials of new treatments.

Research and development

11.13 Advances in science and technology have revolutionised modern medicine, providing the antibiotics, vaccines, modern anaesthetics and pharmaceuticals that have helped transform our lives. The NHS has a responsibility to contribute to, facilitate and embrace these advances in partnership with the private and charitable sectors and academia. We will lead this by further developing a strong set of national research and development programmes. However, we recognise that this top-level commitment needs all staff and their organisations to be involved in developing innovative ways of improving patient care.

11.14 We now have the first provisional map of the human genome and innovation will occur at an ever faster rate. It is vital that the NHS plays an active and collaborative role in realising the benefits in genetics. We will contribute with other government departments and medical charities to a long-term study of the interactions of genetics and the environment in common diseases of adults such as cancer, heart disease and diabetes. These powerful techniques for understanding and treating disease also raise important issues for society in general. The Government has already set up the Human Genetics Commission to advise on the social, ethical and legal implications of developments in genetics and to engage the public in considering these questions.

11.15 Working with the private sector and other partners we will commission NHS research and development in new centres of excellence. These medical knowledge parks will evaluate all aspects of the emerging developments in genetics, from the laboratory testing to the requirement for counselling of patients. They will bring together NHS research, the private and charitable sectors alongside front-line NHS staff and patients.

NHSplus

11.16 Working with the private sector is not just a one-way arrangement. The NHS also has a lot to offer industry and employers; ill health has a big effect on the economy. It has a cost in terms of lost productivity and – where the illness is severe or debilitating – can result in unemployment which in turn is a principal cause of poverty.

11.17 A total of almost a quarter of a million working years are lost through disease each year. The Confederation of British Industry estimates that temporary sickness costs business over £10 billion annually. The burden is born by employers and by the NHS too. Backpain accounts for 119 million days of certified incapacity. It also consumes 12 million GP consultations and 800,000 in-patient days of hospital care.

11.18 Individuals, business and government all have an interest then, in breaking the vicious cycle of illness, unemployment and poverty. Across the country, the NHS is already working in partnership with private sector employers to improve the health of their employees. There are managers receiving NHS pre-employment checks, other staff benefiting from NHS health checks, and a range of advice being given by the NHS on health and safety, health information, risk assessment, environmental health advice and stress management. Services of this sort are of particular benefit for small and medium-sized enterprises which lack the size to organise in-house services but where ill health amongst employees can have serious consequences. The NHS gets the benefit too, by intervening to prevent and avoid injuries and sickness before they occur.

Addenbrookes Hospital NHS Trust and Royal Berkshire and Battle Hospital NHS Trust currently make occupational health services available to small and medium sized enterprises in their areas – and cover their costs by charging employers for these services. Sandwell Healthcare NHS Trust is now working with small and medium-sized businesses to provide early assessment and intervention for workplace back pain. Salisbury Healthcare NHS Trust is working with 300 local businesses in partnership with the local Chamber of Commerce.

11.19 These partnerships will be extended. A new set of services, NHSplus, will be developed as part of this NHS Plan. A portfolio of NHS occupational health services will be identified which can then be bought, in whole or in part, by employers to improve the health of their employees.

11.20 NHSplus will be established as a national agency. The business plan for NHSplus will ensure these new services are provided at no cost to the taxpayer and will build upon local services provided by hospitals and Primary Care Trusts. Surpluses will be reinvested in the expansion and improvement of NHS services. NHSplus will be launched in 2001 and its coverage will develop as the capacity of the NHS expands.

Conclusion

11.21 A closer working relationship between the NHS and the private and voluntary sector will be mutually beneficial. By putting the relationship on a new footing NHS patients will benefit. It will, in particular, contribute to winning the war on waiting for treatment in the NHS.

12

Cutting waiting for treatment

- one-stop out-of-hours services
- GP appointments within 48 hours
- an end to long trolley waits
- accident and emergency waiting times cut
- three months maximum wait for outpatients by 2005
- six months maximum wait for an operation by 2005 falling to three months thereafter
- treatment according to urgency and individual need within these new maximum waiting times

Introduction

12.1   The public's top concern about the NHS is waiting for treatment. Waiting to see a GP, waiting to be seen in a casualty department, waiting to get into hospital and, sometimes, waiting to get out of hospital. A combination of investment and reform will allow progress on each of these fronts.

Primary care

12.2   By the end of 2000 NHS Direct, the 24-hour telephone helpline, will have gone nationwide. By 2004 it will be providing health information via digital TV as well as via the telephone and internet. By then there will be over 500 NHS Direct information points providing touch-screen information and advice about health and the health service in places like shopping centres and railway stations.

12.3   Starting in 2001, patients will get greater access to authoritative information about how they can care for themselves and their families under the aegis of NHSplus which will produce and kitemark books, leaflets and other written material.

12.4   By 2001, there will be new quality standards and closer integration too between NHS Direct and GP out-of-hours services. By 2004 a single phone call to NHS Direct will be a one-stop gateway to out-of-hours healthcare, passing on calls, where necessary, to the appropriate GP co-operative or deputising service.

12.5   By 2002 all NHS Direct sites will refer people, where appropriate, to help from their local pharmacy. There will be better out-of-hours pharmacy services and a wider range of over-the-counter medicines available. By 2004 every primary care group or trust will have schemes in place so that people get more help from pharmacists in using their medicines. There will be repeat dispensing schemes nationwide to make obtaining repeat prescriptions easier for patients with chronic conditions. These changes will speed up services and help relieve pressures on GP surgeries.

12.6   By 2004, patients will be able to see a primary care professional within 24 hours, and a GP within 48 hours. Half of all practices already achieve this target as a result of careful organisation. In future, all practices will be required to guarantee this level of access for their patients, either by providing the service themselves, or by entering into an arrangement with another practice, or by the introduction of further NHS walk-in centres.

12.7   By 2004 patients who currently have to go to hospital will be able to have tests and treatment in primary care centres as staff numbers and skills expand:

- by 2004 consultants who previously worked only in hospitals will be delivering approximately 4 million outpatient consultations in primary care and community settings

- up to 1,000 specialist GPs will be taking referrals from fellow GPs for conditions in specialties such as ophthalmology, orthopaedics, dermatology and ear nose and throat surgery. They will also be able to undertake diagnostic procedures such as endoscopy.

Dentistry

12.8   The Government is firmly committed to making high quality NHS dentistry available to all who want it by September 2001. The initiatives we have taken since 1997 have already made a real difference but more needs to be done. In future, NHS Direct will help direct patients to NHS dentistry. The Government will fund more dental access centres and improvements to dental practices. It will reward dentists' commitment to the NHS and foster better quality services for patients, making NHS dentistry a modern and truly national service again. Health authorities will take the lead in delivering the changes which patients expect.

Intermediate care

12.9   By 2004 we will end widespread bed blocking. All parts of the country will have new intermediate care services which will be underpinned by new arrangements to ensure more seamless care for patients. We will introduce new standards to ensure every patient has a discharge plan including an assessment of their care needs, developed from the beginning of their hospital admission. Together these measures mean that patients should not have their discharge from hospital delayed because they are awaiting assessment, support at home (adaptation, equipment or package of care), or suitable intermediate or other NHS care.

Hospital care

12.10 By 2004 no-one should be waiting more than four hours in accident and emergency from arrival to admission, transfer or discharge. Average waiting times in accident and emergency will fall as a result to 75 minutes. By then we will have ended inappropriate trolley waits for assessment and admission. Of course some patients such as those emergencies arriving by ambulance will clinically need to be assessed on a trolley, but after that if they need a hospital bed they should be admitted to one without undue delay.

12.11 This will involve major changes to the way that hospitals work. It may require more staff and the creation of medical assessment and admissions units in all hospitals that do not have them. It will require new working practices, with nurses taking on new roles including the right to admit patients and order diagnostic procedures. Patients with minor injuries will often be treated by appropriately trained primary care staff working in accident and emergency departments. The new Modernisation Agency will work with hospitals to spread best practice in accident and emergency services.

New maximum waiting times

12.12 Waiting for treatment has been part and parcel of the way the NHS has worked since its formation. It will require fundamental and comprehensive reform to tackle this problem.

12.13 At present the average wait to see a consultant for an outpatient appointment is seven weeks and the average time that people have been waiting for an operation is three months. But some people wait much longer than this – up to 18 months for inpatient treatment – and it is this which so concerns the public.

12.14 There are several reasons for long waiting times:

- as earlier parts of this Plan explained the NHS has not had the resources, equipment and the staff to carry out enough treatments and operations

- there have been particular problems with some conditions – for example, four specialties account for most of the long waits: orthopaedics, dermatology, ear, nose and throat problems and eye conditions

- at a national level waiting lists have been the NHS' way of balancing supply and demand – of matching the volume of care it can provide to the number of people wanting treatment. And at a local level waiting lists have been the way of ensuring that consultants always have a flow of patients to treat

- the systems for taking patients through the hospital system have been outdated and inefficient. Too many patients get sent to the wrong part of the system. Tests, results and diagnosis are not matched up to provide a complete and integrated service. The scheduling of clinics and theatre lists has been wasteful. And too many operations have been cancelled.

12.15 Each of these problems will be tackled as part of a war on waiting. As chapters 4 and 5 described, the NHS Plan will see year on year increases in equipment, facilities and staff. As the extra capacity comes on stream so we will be able to reduce waiting times. Those areas where there are particular problems will be targeted for special action – though it will take time to get the right supply of consultants and other staff into each specialty.

12.16 The introduction of on-the-spot booking systems will not just make getting a hospital appointment more convenient for patients. It also acts as a driver of much more fundamental reform. Booking appointments forces hospitals to organise their clinic slots and theatre sessions much more productively. It also brings a dramatic reduction in the number of cancelled appointments and the occasions when patients just do not turn up.

12.17 The booked appointment system also ensures that consultants have a regular scheduled stream of work. In addition, it involves GPs and hospital consultants sitting down and agreeing the basis on which referrals should be made and which services would best be carried out in the surgery and which in hospital. That in turn helps to make it more likely that consultants will spend their time seeing patients who have been referred appropriately.

12.18 So booking drives reform at several different levels. Booking is part and parcel of the wider and more radical process, described in chapter 6, of redesigning services round the patient, cutting out unnecessary stages of treatment, using staff more flexibly and reducing delays.

12.19 By increasing investment and making reforms the NHS Plan will be able to deliver major reductions in waiting times covering all stages of acute care. Within new guaranteed maximum waiting time backstops, patients will be treated according to individual clinicians' assessment of clinical urgency and need.

12.20 By the end of 2005:

- waiting lists for hospital appointments and admission will be abolished and replaced with booking systems giving all patients a choice of a convenient time within a guaranteed maximum waiting time. As a first step towards this all hospitals will by April 2001 have booking systems in place covering two procedures within their major specialties

- assuming GP referrals remain broadly in line with the current trend in the growth of referrals, then the maximum waiting time for a routine outpatient appointment will be halved from over six months now to three months – urgent cases will continue to be treated much faster in accordance with clinical need. As a result of delivering this policy we would expect the average time for an outpatient appointment to fall to five weeks

- the maximum wait for inpatient treatment will be cut from 18 months now to six months. Urgent cases will continue to be treated much faster in accordance with clinical need. As a result of delivering this policy we would expect the average time that patients have been waiting for inpatient treatment to fall from three months to seven weeks.

12.21 Our eventual objective is to reduce the maximum wait for any stage of treatment to three months. Provided that we can recruit the extra staff, and the NHS makes the necessary reforms, we hope to achieve the objective by the end of 2008.

12.22 We will progress towards our objectives on a staged basis – the pace of progress being linked to the growth in staff. The Plan will see a staged reduction of maximum inpatient waits from 18 months through 15, 12, 9 down to 6, and eventually 3 months.

Conclusion

12.23 Expansion in staff alongside reforms to the way local health services are organised will deliver the most sustained assault on waiting the NHS has ever seen. The pace of progress is dependent upon the growth in staff. But by the end of 2005 waiting times at all stages in a patient's care will have fallen dramatically.

13

Improving health and reducing inequality

- a national health inequalities target
- increased resources in deprived areas
- new screening programmes
- world-leading smoking cessation services
- free fruit for infant schoolchildren

Introduction

13.1   No injustice is greater than the inequalities in health which scar our nation. The life expectancy of a boy born into the bottom social class is over nine years less than a boy born into the most affluent social class. The gap between health needs and health services remains stubbornly wide.

13.2   The worst health problems in our country will not be tackled without dealing with their fundamental causes. This means tackling disadvantage in all its forms – poverty, lack of educational attainment, unemployment, discrimination and social exclusion. It means recognising the specific health needs of different groups, including people with disabilities and minority ethnic groups. Improving health is now a key priority for all government departments. Action will be taken to step up the cross-governmental focus on health and inequalities.

13.3   The NHS too has a stronger role to play in prevention, as well as working in partnership with other agencies to tackle the causes of ill health so as to reduce health inequalities.

Setting a national inequalities target

13.4   The White Paper – *Saving Lives: Our Healthier Nation* – required the setting of local targets for reducing health inequalities. For the first time ever, local targets will now be reinforced by the creation of national health inequalities targets, to narrow the health gap in childhood and throughout life between socio-economic groups and between the most deprived areas and the rest of the country. Specific targets will be developed in consultation with external stakeholders and expert advice, as the new national statistics classification becomes available early in 2001.

13.5   In particular, we will set a target to narrow the longstanding gap in infant and early childhood mortality and morbidity between socio-economic groups as well as a target to address inequalities later in life.

13.6   These inequalities targets will be delivered by a combination of specific health policies and broader government policies, including abolishing child poverty, expanding Sure Start and action on cancer and coronary heart disease.

13.7   To underpin this national work on cutting inequalities we will by 2002 develop a new health poverty index that combines data about health status, access to health services, uptake of preventive services and the opportunities to pursue and maintain good health (eg access to affordable nutritious food, physical activity and a safe, clean environment).

Reducing inequalities in access to NHS services

13.8   'The inverse care law', where communities in greatest need are least likely to receive the health services that they require, still applies in too many parts of the country. Inequity in access to services is not restricted to social class and geography; people in minority ethnic communities are less likely to receive the services they need. Many deprived communities are less likely than affluent ones to receive heart surgery, hip replacements and many other services including screening.

13.9   By 2003, following the review of the existing weighted capitation formula used to distribute NHS funding, reducing inequalities will be a key criterion for allocating NHS resources to different parts of the country.

13.10   Linked to this there will be a new way of distributing resources to address inequities in primary care services. They have historically been excluded from the NHS 'weighted capitation' formula. Instead, the Medical Practices Committee (MPC) has sought to ensure the fair distribution of GPs across the NHS, with only partial success. For example there are 50% more GPs in Kingston and Richmond or Oxfordshire than there are in Barnsley or Sunderland after adjusting for the age and needs of their respective populations.

13.11   In future, the new Medical Education Standards Board (see chapter 8) will track the number and distribution of doctors in primary care. The Medical Practices Committee will be abolished and replaced with a single resource allocation formula covering all NHS spending including general medical services non-cash limited (GMSNCL) expenditure. Progress to new targets will be on the basis of a proper 'pace of change' policy. This will both improve equity and allow more flexible models of primary care services.

13.12 To improve further the equitable distribution of GPs and primary care staff, there will be 200 new Personal Medical Services schemes created principally in disadvantaged communities by 2004. New incentives will be developed to help recruit and retain good staff in disadvantaged areas. Health centres in the most deprived communities will be modernised.

13.13 By 2001 local NHS action on tackling health inequalities and ensuring equitable access to healthcare will for the first time be measured and managed through the NHS Performance Assessment Framework. The NHS will need to address local inequalities including issues such as access to services for black and ethnic minority communities.

13.14 By 2003 a free and nationally available translationand interpretation service will be available from every NHS premises through NHS Direct.

Children: ensuring a healthy start in life

13.15 Health at the very beginning of life is the foundation for health throughout life. It is now recognised that women's health in infancy can affect the health of their children. Although infant mortality rates have improved over recent years the English rate remains above the European average. Infant mortality rates vary widely across health authorities in England, with the highest health authority rate being three and a half times that of the lowest rate. There are also large variations in infant mortality rates by social class of father and ethnic origin of mother. Infants born to fathers in unskilled or semi-skilled occupations have a mortality rate 1.6 times higher than those in professional or managerial occupations. And children of women born in Pakistan are twice as likely to die in their first year than children of women born in the UK.

13.16 By 2004 there will be:

- a big expansion of Sure Start projects to cover a third of children aged under four years living in poverty. Spending will rise to around £500 million. This will help break the cycle of deprivation through early sustained intervention to promote health, social, and emotional development as well as educational attainment

- the creation of the new Children's Fund worth £450 million over three years

- a reform of the welfare foods programme to use the resources more effectively to ensure children in poverty have access to a healthy diet, and increased support for breast feeding and parenting

- full implementation of the Government's teenage pregnancy strategy, bringing about a 15% reduction in the rate of teenage conceptions, consistent with the longer term target of reducing the rate of teenage conception by half by 2010

- effective and appropriate screening programmes for women and children including a new national linked antenatal and neonatal screening programme for haemoglobinopathy and sickle cell disease

- a new sexual health and HIV strategy to improve access to and links between services, to introduce new screening programmes, to spread good practice and to ensure standards for primary and secondary prevention.

Reducing smoking

13.17 Seven in ten smokers want to give up, but smoking kills 120,000 people a year. It is the leading single cause of avoidable ill health and early death. It is the biggest single cause of the difference in death rates between rich and poor. Smoking in pregnancy reduces birth weight, and contributes to perinatal mortality. To boost the measures set out in the White Paper *Smoking Kills* – which include a ban on tobacco advertising and sponsorship – the NHS Plan sets out a major expansion in smoking cessation to give England a world-leading service.

13.18 By 2001:

- for the first time, the NHS will provide a comprehensive smoking cessation service. Nicotine replacement therapy (NRT) will be available on prescription from GPs, to complement the newly available smoking cessation treatment, buproprion (Zyban)

- the National Institute for Clinical Excellence will be asked to advise GPs on the most appropriate and cost-effective prescribing regimes for nicotine replacement therapy and buproprion, including duration and targeting

- the Committee on Safety of Medicines will also be asked to consider whether nicotine replacement therapy can be made available for general sale rather than only through pharmacies or on prescription

- specialist smoking cessation services will focus on heavily dependent smokers needing intensive support, and on pregnant smokers as part of ante-natal care. primary care groups will take the lead in commissioning – and where appropriate providing – these services, in support of the new smoking cessation treatments now to be prescribable at practice level.

13.19 The success of this programme will mean that by 2010, approximately 55,000 fewer women will be smoking in pregnancy: a major contribution to tackling health inequalities and improving infant mortality. By 2010 at least 1.5 million smokers will have given up smoking.

Improving diet and nutrition

13.20 Poor nutrition leads to low birth weight and poor weight gain in the first year of life, which in turn contributes to the later development of disease, particularly heart disease. Increasing fruit and vegetable consumption is considered the second most effective strategy to reduce the risk of cancer, after reducing smoking, and it has major preventive benefits for heart disease too. Eating at least five portions of fruit and vegetables a day could lead to estimated reductions of up to 20% in overall deaths from chronic diseases. In the UK, average consumption is only about three portions a day, and a fifth of children eat no fruit in a week. Information is important, but the food choices people can make are shaped by the availability and affordability of food locally.

13.21 People make their own choices about what to eat. The role of Government is to ensure people have information and proper access to healthy food wherever they live. So by 2004 action will include:

- a new National School Fruit Scheme where every child in nursery and aged four to six in infant schools will be entitled to a free piece of fruit each school day, as part of a national campaign to improve the diet of children. We will examine the practicalities of the scheme through pilots before rolling it out nationally

- a five-a-day programme to increase fruit and vegetable consumption

- work with industry – including producers as well as retailers – to increase provision and access to fruit and vegetables with local initiatives, where necessary, to establish local food co-operatives

- initiatives with the food industry – including manufacturers and caterers – to improve the overall balance of diet including salt, fat and sugar in food, working with the Food Standards Agency

- local action to tackle obesity and physical inactivity, informed by advice from the new Health Development Agency on what works

- a hospital nutrition policy to improve the outcome of care for patients. This will also reduce dependency on intravenous feeding regimes.

Tackling drugs and alcohol-related crime

There are up to 200,000 problem drug misusers in the UK, of whom no more than half are in contact with treatment services. There are up to 2,300 drug-related deaths a year and this figure has been rising since 1980. With other government departments, we are committed to reducing the proportion of people under the age of 25 reporting the use of class A drugs by 25% by 2005 and 50% by 2008. We are also committed to increasing the number of problem drug misusers in treatment by 66% by 2005, and 100% by 2008. We will do this by:

- targeting education and prevention activity to intervene before people develop the habits which do so much damage

- strengthening treatment services for drug misusers by setting up a new National Treatment Agency accountable to the Department of Health. It will have a budget that pools resources spent on services for drug misusers, from health and other agencies

- by 2004 we will be implementing a strategy to address alcohol misuse which causes 30,000 early deaths a year.

New partnerships to tackle inequality

13.22 The NHS cannot tackle health inequalities alone. The wider determinants of ill health and inequality call for a new partnership between health and local services. That is the key strategic role for health authorities.

13.23 The NHS will play a full part in the Government's National Strategy for Neighbourhood Renewal supported by £800 million over three years.

13.24 The NHS will help develop Local Strategic Partnerships, into which, in the medium term, health action zones and other local action zones could be integrated to strengthen the links between health, education, employment and other causes of social exclusion. In the meantime effective health action zones will continue.

13.25 By 2002 there will be new single, integrated, public health groups across NHS regional offices and government offices of the regions. Accountable through the regional director of public health jointly to the director of the government office for the region and the NHS regional director, they will enable regeneration of regions to embrace health as well as environment, transport and inward investment.

13.26 By 2002 there will be a Healthy Communities Collaborative to spread best practice under the aegis of the new Modernisation Agency using evidence from the Health Development Agency and the successful formula already in place in the Cancer Collaborative and the Primary Care Collaborative.

13.27 By 2003 there will be a leadership programme for health visitors and community nurses under the new NHS Leadership Centre to provide them with the skills and expertise to work directly with representatives of local neighbourhood and housing estates to support communities to improve health.

Conclusion

13.28 These changes will help embed work on prevention and health inequalities within the core of what the NHS does. Opening up opportunities for all to decent health and a decent health service will take time. But over the next few years we intend to make progress. These efforts will be given new impetus by tackling our country's biggest killer diseases – cancer and coronary heart disease.

14

The clinical priorities

- a big expansion in cancer screening programmes
- an end to the postcode lottery in the prescibing of cancer drugs
- rapid access chest pain clinics across the country by 2003
- shorter waits for heart operations
- 335 mental health teams to provide an immediate response to crises

Introduction

14.1 Action will be taken to tackle a wide range of conditions and diseases. Improving health and tackling inequalities requires investment and reform in key services: coronary heart disease, cancer and mental health (together with elderly care services – see chapter 15). Heart disease and cancer are our biggest killers. Mental health services suffered from decades of neglect despite the huge numbers of people affected by mental illness. In each case expansion and reform is needed to bring about improvements for patients.

Cancer

14.2 Cancer kills 100,000 people a year. Unskilled workers are twice as likely to die from the disease as professionals. And although survival rates have improved over the past 30 years, they are worse for several common cancers than in equivalent European countries.

14.3 The *Our Healthier Nation* White Paper set out our commitment to cut the death rate from cancer in people under 75 by at least a fifth by 2010, aiming, in particular, to improve the health of the worst off. We have invested additional resources to improve services for breast, colorectal, lung and gynaecological cancers in line with evidence-based guidance. We are reducing outpatient waits for urgent referrals, and have embarked on the biggest ever programme to replace and update screening, diagnosis and treatment equipment. This autumn we will publish a National Cancer Plan to improve cancer services across the whole country.

Investment

14.4 Extra investment, improved prevention, and changed ways of working will mean that cancer services will improve up to and beyond 2005, so that by 2010 our five year cancer survival rates will compare with the best in Europe. We will be investing an extra £570 million a year in cancer services by 2003/04. There will be substantial investment in extra specialist cancer staff. The six medical specialties that contribute most substantially to cancer services, for example, will increase by 24% by 2003/04. There will be similar increases in other specialties relevant to cancer. Further expansion will follow.

Prevention

14.5 The action we set out in the previous chapter to reduce smoking (which accounts for about a third of all cancer deaths), and to improve diet (which accounts for a further quarter) will be central to our efforts to improve cancer services. But we need to go further still. Over the next few years we will extend existing screening programmes, and introduce new screening programmes for other cancers, as evidence about their effectiveness and benefit is confirmed:

- the NHS breast screening programme, which currently covers women aged 50-64, will be extended to women aged 65-70. The current service will be upgraded by offering two view mammography, leading to an estimated 40% improvement in detection rates. Expanding the programme will require a 40% increase in skilled staff. For this reason, new skill mix arrangements, including a new grade of assistant practitioner, will be piloted from September and extended quickly thereafter. Some 400,000 more women will be screened each year when the programme is fully implemented

- the cervical cancer screening programme will be upgraded by introducing cost-effective new screening technologies, benefiting the four million women covered each year by the programme. Unnecessary repeat smears will be reduced and access to further tests for those who need them improved

- as pilot studies demonstrate that colorectal cancer screening is appropriate, feasible and acceptable to the public, a national screening programme will be established

- if and when screening and treatment techniques have developed sufficiently, a prostate cancer screening programme will be introduced. The evidence to support the introduction of a screening programme will be kept under careful review by the National Screening Committee. A Prostate Cancer Action Plan encompassing research, diagnosis, early detection, treatment and care, will be built into the National Cancer Plan to be published in autumn 2000.

14.6 Screening programmes will be extended to other cancers such as ovarian cancer as and when research demonstrates that screening is appropriate and cost effective.

Research

14.7 A new NHS Cancer Research Network will be fully implemented by 2004. Its initial aim is to double the total proportion of adult cancer patients entering trials within three years. An extra £5 million per annum will fund it from 2001/02.

14.8 Further specific plans for cancer research will be outlined in the National Cancer Plan later this year. However, we are already committed to increasing by £1 million the resources devoted to prostate cancer for each of the next three years.

Access to services

14.9 A 'Cancer Services Collaborative' is working with nine cancer networks across the country to streamline all stages in the pathway of care. The new Modernisation Agency will extend this approach to all cancer networks by 2003. The National Cancer Plan will contain referral to diagnosis to treatment waiting times targets, to be drawn up in discussion with clinicians and patient groups, taking account of the speed at which the workforce can expand.

14.10 The extra investment we are making in equipment to diagnose and treat cancer (see paragraph 4.13) will benefit over 400,000 patients every year.

14.11 Over the next year the National Institute for Clinical Excellence will be assessing a wide range of anti-cancer drugs and will issue guidance to the NHS by summer 2001 on their clinical and cost effectiveness. The funding we are making available will mean the NHS is able to implement the National Institute for Clinical Excellence's recommendations, tackling the postcode prescribing lottery for cancer drugs. Some 30,000 people can be confident as a result that they will receive newly licensed drugs, where this is clinically appropriate.

14.12 The National Institute for Clinical Excellence will issue guidance by 2002 on how best to organise urological, haemotological, and head and neck cancer services and supportive/palliative care. It will also update existing guidance for breast, bowel, and lung cancer services. Implementation will be rolled out as the guidance becomes available. Some 55,000 patients a year will benefit. By 2005 authoritative guidance will be available from the National Institute for Clinical Excellence on new standards for all aspects of NHS cancer care, with implementation taking place in line with the expansion in the workforce.

Conclusion

14.13 Taken together, these plans should mean that England will have the fastest improvement in cancer services across Europe over the next 5 years.

Coronary heart disease

14.14 Coronary heart disease is common, frequently fatal, and largely preventable. The burden of heart disease is higher and has fallen less in the UK than in many other countries. It kills more than 110,000 people a year in England. Death rates are three times higher among manual workers than among managers.

14.15 The Coronary Heart Disease National Service Framework, published earlier this year, for the first time set out a ten year programme to transform the prevention, diagnosis, treatment and care of patients with heart disease. When it is fully implemented 20,000 lives a year should be saved. The extra investment going into the NHS will allow it to be implemented more speedily.

Investment

14.16 We shall be investing an extra £230 million a year in heart disease services by 2003/04. There will also be an extra £120 million of capital funding from the Treasury Capital Modernisation Fund over the two years to March 2002, to expand capacity and modernise services.

14.17 Investment will be channelled into expanding the workforce, especially consultants. The number of cardiologists will increase by some 10% each year from 1999/2000, building to a total of some 685 by 2003/04: an increase of 47%. Numbers of trainees currently in the pipeline means that cardiothoracic surgeons will increase by some 4.5% each year for the next few years – an increase of 19% by 2003/04. But further expansion will follow as more trainees move through into consultant posts.

Prevention

14.18 Action on smoking (see paragraph 13.15-13.17) will have a dramatic impact on rates of coronary heart disease. So too will better provision of coronary heart disease services in primary care. In future, all patients with established heart disease or at significant risk of developing it will receive advice and treatment to reduce their risk of death, heart attack, heart failure and other problems. By 2003 all practices will have disease management registers in place, will be actively managing patients at risk of coronary heart disease, and should have clinical audit data that demonstrates this.

14.19 Over one million patients with established heart disease, or at high risk, will benefit from these improvements in care. More effective prescribing will save lives: over 1,000 lives a year just from prescribing aspirin to heart attack survivors and 3,000 lives a year from prescribing statins to people at significant risk.

Treatment

14.20 At present thousands of patients can wait months to see a heart specialist in order to get an assessment and firm diagnosis. So by 2003 rapid access chest pain clinics will be established right across the country to assess, within two weeks, all patients with new onset chest pain which their GP thinks might be due to angina. There will be 50 such clinics by April 2001, 100 by April 2002, with national roll-out being completed in 2003. By then 200,000 patients a year will be receiving early diagnosis. Cardiac rehabilitation services will be expanded too.

14.21 At present, thousands of lives are unnecessarily lost each year because of delays in treating heart attack patients. Clot-busting drugs (thrombolysis) should be given within 60 minutes of calling for professional help yet this only happens in about one case in ten. There will be three reforms to improve 'call-to-needle' times:

- the immediate priority is to improve ambulance response times because every minute counts – arriving one minute earlier after heart attack gives an extra 11 days of life. By 2001 the ambulance service should achieve a first response to 75% of Category A calls within 8 minutes. This progress on ambulance response times will save up to 1,800 lives a year

- by 2003, 75% of eligible people will receive thrombolysis within 20 minutes of hospital arrival as services are redesigned

- there will be a three year programme to train and equip ambulance paramedics to provide thrombolysis safely for appropriate patients. On average, patients will get thrombolysis an hour sooner than if they were taken to hospital first, saving up to 3,000 lives a year once fully implemented.

14.22 Waiting times for cardiac surgery will be cut. The NHS underprovides cardiac surgery so waiting times are too long. Currently, there are some 450 coronary artery by-pass grafts (CABGs) per million population carried out in the NHS per annum and some 375 percutaneous transluminal coronary angioplasty (PTCAs), against a National Service Framework target of at least 750 per million of each procedure per annum. For that reason the National Service Framework set out a series of staged aims to expand capacity and reduce waits as fast as the expansion of staffing will permit.

14.23 The National Service Framework pledged an expansion of 3,000 extra heart operations in the two years to March 2002 at a cost of £50 million. We shall now boost this with a further £10 million in the current year backed by £120 million over two years from the Treasury Capital Modernisation Fund, to support more rapid expansion of existing services and begin the development of new cardiac centres. This will enable the NHS to achieve the 3,000 target ahead of time, and to bring on stream at least a further 3,000 operations on top of this by 2003.

14.24 This programme of expansion will mean that the maximum waiting times for routine cardiac surgery will fall to a 6 months backstop by 2005 and to the National Service Framework goal of a 3 months maximum wait by 2008.

Service redesign

14.25 The Coronary Heart Disease Partnership Programme, starting in October 2000, will work with a group of cardiac networks across the country to streamline the delivery of high quality, patient-centred care and get the most out of existing capacity. This will build on the experience of the Cancer Services Collaborative and will complement the work of the Primary Care Development Team. The lessons learnt from the Partnership Programme will be rolled out right across the country by 2004.

Conclusion

14.26 Decades of underinvestment in coronary heart disease services will come to an end. Extra resources and new ways of working should, by 2008, give England heart disease services that rival the best in Europe.

Mental health

14.27 Modernising mental health services is one of the Government's core national priorities. We have already set out a ten year programme to put in place new standards of care. Extra investment already committed will allow us to create, by April next year, almost 500 extra secure beds, over 320 24-hour staffed beds, 170 assertive outreach teams and access to services 24 hours a day, seven days a week, for all those with complex mental health needs. The priority has been to ensure that people with severe and enduring mental illness receive services that are more responsive to their needs.

14.28 This Plan now provides an extra annual investment of over £300 million by 2003/04 to fast forward the National Service Framework.

Primary care

14.29 Most mental health problems are managed in primary care. One in four GP consultations are with people with mental health problems. So improving these services will have a major impact on the health and wellbeing of the population:

- one thousand new graduate primary care mental health workers, trained in brief therapy techniques of proven effectiveness, will be employed to help GPs manage and treat common mental health problems in all age groups, including children. In addition, 500 more community mental health staff will be employed to work with general practitioners and primary care teams, with NHS Direct, and in each accident and emergency department to respond to people who need immediate help. These staff will be able to call on crisis resolution teams if necessary

- by 2004, more than 300,000 people will receive extra help from the new primary care mental health workers and around 500,000 people will benefit from additional mental health staff working in frontline settings. These changes will ease pressure on GP services.

Early intervention in psychosis

14.30 Early intervention to reduce the period of untreated psychosis in young people can prevent initial problems, and improve long-term outcomes:

- fifty early intervention teams will therefore be established over the next three years to provide treatment and active support in the community to these young people and their families

- by 2004 all young people who experience a first episode of psychosis, such as schizophrenia, will receive the early and intensive support they need. This will benefit 7,500 young people each year.

Crisis resolution

14.31 At the moment the only option in many areas is to admit people with an acute mental illness to hospital. Crisis resolution teams respond quickly to people in crisis, providing assessment and treatment wherever they are:

- a total of 335 teams will be established over the next three years

- by 2004, all people in contact with specialist mental health services will be able to access crisis resolution services at any time. The teams will treat around 100,000 people a year who would otherwise have to be admitted to hospital, including black and South Asian service users for whom this type of service has been shown to be particularly beneficial. Pressure on acute inpatient units will be reduced by 30% and there will generally be no out of area admissions which are not clinically indicated.

Assertive outreach services

14.32 There are a small number of people who are difficult to engage. They are very high users of services, and often suffer from a dual diagnosis of substance misuse and serious mental illness. A small proportion also have a history of offending. Services to provide assertive outreach and intensive input seven days a week are required to sustain engagement with services, and to protect patient and public:

- a further 50 teams will be established over the next three years in addition to the 170 teams which will be in place by next April

- by 2003 all 20,000 people estimated to need assertive outreach will be receiving these services.

Services for women

14.33 Mental health services are not always sensitive to the needs of women. Yet women are more likely to suffer from mental health problems, particularly anxiety, depression and eating disorders. One in ten women have postnatal depression after childbirth:

- by 2004, services will be redesigned to ensure there are women-only day centres in every health authority compared with only a handful at present.

Support for carers

14.34 When asked, the vast majority of carers focus on the need for mental health services to be provided around the clock. But in addition, carers require time out to reduce the risk of social isolation which tends to go with caring, especially caring for someone with severe mental illness:

- by 2004, 700 more staff will be recruited to increase the breaks available for carers, and to strengthen carer support networks. There are very few such staff at present. By then around 165,000 carers will be receiving the support they need to continue to provide care.

High secure hospitals

14.35 Some 300-400 patients in high secure hospitals do not require that level of security but remain there because no suitable alternative place is available. The Government has recently announced an additional £25 million to develop 200 long-term secure beds to allow patients to move on, and to employ 400 additional community staff to provide intensive support when patients are eventually discharged. By 2004, up to 400 patients should have moved from the high secure hospitals to more appropriate accommodation.

Prison services

14.36 At any time some 5,000 people with a serious mental illness will be in prison. It is important to improve the health screening of those received into custody and to identify and provide treatment for prisoners with mental health problems. Within the new partnerships between the NHS and local prisons, some 300 additional staff will be employed.

- by 2004, 5000 prisoners at any time should be receiving more comprehensive mental health services in prison. All people with severe mental illness will be in receipt of treatment, and no prisoner with serious mental illness will leave prison without a care plan and a care co-ordinator.

New structures

14.37 To ensure that mental health and social care provision can be properly integrated locally, statutory powers will be taken to permit the establishment of combined mental health and social care trusts. Every such trust will be required to establish a Patient Advocate and Liaison Service (see paragraph 10.17).

14.38 The Mental Health Act (1993) will be reformed to create a new legislative framework reflecting modern patterns of care and treatment for severe mental illness. The focus will be on managing risk and providing better health outcomes for patients.

14.39 The Government is also considering proposals for those people with severe personality disorder who present a high risk to the public. By 2004, an additional 140 new secure places and 75 specialist rehabilitation hostel places will be provided for people with severe personality disorder employing almost 400 extra staff.

Conclusion

14.40 New investment, combined with major reforms, will modernise mental health, cancer and coronary heart disease services. Thousands of patients will feel the benefits of improving services, better geared to meeting their needs. The same combination of expansion and reform will improve services for older people as well.

15

Dignity, security and independence in old age

Introduction

15.1 Older people make up the largest single group of patients using the NHS. People over 65 account for two-thirds of hospital patients and 40% of all emergency admissions. Too often they are treated in inappropriate acute hospital settings because there is nowhere else. Older people also worry about the prospect of deteriorating health, and can be anxious that they may not receive the care they need, sometimes simply because of their age. They are also distressed when service providers fail to respect their dignity and privacy – a problem which can occur at home or in a nursing home, as well as on the hospital ward. There can be particular problems for those from black and minority ethnic communities in accessing the services which meet their needs and wishes.

15.2 This is the generation that has supported the NHS all their lives. This Plan sets out a major package of investment, to improve services and standards of care for older people. By 2004 the Government is making available annually an additional £1.4 billion for new investment in health and social services for older people.

15.3 We know from listening to older people that they want health and social services that will put them, and their needs and wishes, at the centre of service delivery:

- assuring standards of care

- extending access to services

- promoting independence in old age

- ensuring fairness in funding.

15.4   This NHS Plan sets out an ambitious programme to begin to make this a reality for older people and their carers.

Assuring standards

15.5   The new National Care Standards Commission will drive up standards across domiciliary and residential care. It will start its work in 2002. Now we intend to raise the standards of care for older people across the piece – health and social care. Later this year we will publish a new national service framework (NSF) which for the first time will set out clear standards for the services that older people use, including those for stroke, falls and mental health problems. Implementation of the standards will start from 2001.

15.6   The NSF will ensure that ageism is not tolerated in the NHS, with the elimination of any arbitrary policies based on age alone. Major concerns have been expressed about ageism in the NHS, and specifically with respect to resuscitation policies. All NHS organisations will be required to establish and implement local resuscitation policies based on the guidelines published by the British Medical Association, Royal College of Nursing and Resuscitation Council (UK) and to include compliance with these policies in their clinical audit programme. The Commission for Health Improvement will assess progress within its clinical governance reviews.

15.7   Health services in partnership with social services and other agencies will need to recognise the specific needs of older people in caring for them:

- demonstrating proper respect for the autonomy, dignity and privacy of older people

- treating the person, not just the most acute symptoms, by taking account of the full needs of older people, including the importance of good nutrition, maintaining tissue viability and enabling the older person to remain as active as possible while in hospital

- making high quality palliative and supportive care available to those older people who need it

- ensuring good clinical practice which recognises the complexities of caring for older people, for example, by promoting the good practice recommendations contained in the most recent report of the National Confidential Enquiry into Peri-Operative Deaths.

Extending access to services

15.8 By 2001 the NHS will: pilot an NHS retirement health check, a free health check on retirement, to review any current treatment and to identify any further potential health problems. We will work with professional bodies to determine the most appropriate package of measures to include. And breast screening will be extended to cover all women aged 65 to 70 years as soon as possible (see paragraph 14.5).

15.9 Local services will streamline their local assessment processes, recognising the complexity of what some older people require. By April 2002, we will introduce a single assessment process for health and social care, with protocols to be agreed locally between health and social services. Initially this will be introduced for those older people who are most vulnerable, for example, those who live alone or those who are recently bereaved or those recently discharged from hospital or entering residential or nursing care.

15.10 During 2002, each of these older people, and where appropriate their carers, will be involved in agreeing a personal care plan, which they will hold. The personal care plan will document their current package of health and social care, their care co-ordinator, monitoring arrangements, and a list of key contacts for rapid response at home and in emergencies.

15.11 There is an important role for clinical leadership in this area, and we will explore the potential for nurse consultants and for specialist nurses for older people.

15.12 We will also be establishing an entirely new service to benefit older people in particular. Care Direct will provide faster access to care, advice and support. This new service will provide information and advice about health, social care, housing, pensions and benefits by telephone, drop-in centres, on-line and through outreach services.

Promoting independence

15.13 In future, the NHS and local social services should support older people to make a faster recovery from illness, encouraging independence rather than institutional care, and providing reliable, high quality on-going support at home.

15.14 The Plan provides an extra £900 million by 2003/04 for investment in intermediate care and related services to promote independence and improved quality of care for older people. This, along with the additional £150 million made available this year, will:

- promote independence through active recovery and rehabilitation services with an extra 5,000 intermediate care beds and a further 1,700 supported intermediate care places, together benefiting around 150,000 more older people each year

- prevent unnecessary admission to hospital with extra rapid response teams and other forms of admission prevention benefiting around 70,000 more people each year

- enable 50,000 more people to live independently at home through additional home care and other support. In addition, 50% more people will benefit from community equipment services (assistive technology) ranging from simple care equipment and adaptations, like grab rails and pressure relief mattresses, to more sophisticated equipment such as fall alarms and remote sensor devices

- extend carers respite services benefiting a further 75,000 carers and those they care for.

15.15 This will not only improve the care of older people and contribute to the elimination of 'bed blocking'. It will also enable the NHS to operate more efficiently by helping to release acute hospital beds. This should enable extra patients to be treated each year, contributing towards the targets on waiting.

Fairness in funding

15.16 Through this investment in intermediate care, older people will be able to maintain their health and independence much more effectively, and remain in their own homes wherever possible. However, for some people, residential or nursing care is the right option. When this is necessary, we must ensure that the funding of long-term care is fair and promotes rather than obstructs good partnership working across health and social services.

15.17 This is not the case at present. The present system of funding is confusing, complicated and anomalous. People who need nursing care in nursing homes may have to pay for it whereas it is free in every other setting. Many people fear having to sell their own homes to pay for their care. Rather than promoting independence, the present rules often reinforce an older person's dependency.

15.18 In 1997 the Government established a Royal Commission on Long-Term Care, under the chairmanship of Sir Stewart Sutherland to examine these issues and to make proposals for reform. The Government is extremely grateful to Sir Stewart and the Commission members. Many of the Commission's recommendations – such as the establishment of a National Care Standards Commission – have already been actioned. Now we are able to respond to the Commission's proposals on the funding of long term care. A full response to the Royal Commission is being published seperately. We will action the following proposals:

- *from April 2001:* for the first three months from admission to residential and nursing home care, the value of a person's home will be disregarded from the means testing rules. This will give people a breathing space in which to consider their position and allow the possibility of a return home. This will benefit around 30,000 people each year.

The capital limits used when assessing someone's ability to contribute to the costs of their care will be restored to the 1996 value and will be kept under review. These changes will benefit around 20,000 people in residential care homes and nursing homes.

We will, for the first time, issue statutory guidance to councils to reduce the current unacceptable variations in charges for home care. This could benefit many of the 500,000 people who receive home care each year.

- *from October 2001:* subject to a decision by Parliament, nursing care provided in nursing homes will be fully funded by the NHS. People should not be asked to contribute towards the costs of their nursing care. We will introduce legislation this year to make these necessary changes. This will remove a major anomaly in the system of funding long-term care and give the NHS a far stronger incentive to ensure effective rehabilitation for people facing the prospect of long-term care. This change will benefit around 35,000 people at any time, and could save up to £5,000 for a year's stay in a nursing home.

- *from April 2002:* payment of the Residential Allowance will cease for new care home residents and the resources will be transferred to local authorities. At present these resources can encourage councils to place older people in residential care and to select independent sector homes. The individual does not benefit from the money as the local authority usually recoups it. In future this money will be available to promote independence and active rehabilitation for older people.

We will provide extra help and financial support to those who entered residential care before April 1993 by ensuring that local councils become responsible for their assessment, care management and financial support. This change will benefit around 65,000 people. In doing this we will ensure that people cannot be moved against their wishes unless there are compelling reasons to do so. Meanwhile we will change the regulations to allow councils to help older people who entered care before the 1993 community care changes and who face eviction from their care home because they cannot pay the fees.

A new grant to local authorities to expand loan schemes should help ensure no old person will be forced to sell their homes against their will when they go into long term care. The new system will be fairer and clearer.

The Government is committed to consult on regulation of long-term care insurance once a Treasury led committee has reported on how the financial services industry can reassure its customers about the quality and reliability of the products available for financing long-term care. The committee's report will be published shortly as part of this consultation exercise, which will consider whether the impact of regulation would be beneficial and proportionate.

15.19 This response to the recommendations of the Royal Commission on Long Term Care means that by 2004 a further £360 million will be invested to help people meet the costs of their residential and nursing home care.

15.20 In proposing all these changes we have considered carefully all the recommendations of the Royal Commission on Long Term Care. The key proposals are accepted, including that nursing care should be free in all settings and that a National Care Standards Commission should be established. The majority report of the Commission also felt that all personal care in nursing and residential care homes should be free although it acknowledged that accommodation costs should still be means tested. By contrast, a minority note fundamentally disagreed with the idea that taxpayers resources should be used to make personal care free. In fact, personal care has never been free. It has been means tested by social services since 1948 although three quarters of people in nursing and residential care currently receive help with some or all their personal care costs. Actioning the proposal would absorb huge and increasing sums of money without using any of it to increase the range and quality of care available to older people. For that reason it is not supported by the Government. Our proposals will involve spending as much money as the majority report recommended but in ways that will bring greater benefits in terms of health and independence for all older people both now and in the future.

Conclusion

15.21 The Government is making £1.4 billion available in 2004 for new investment in better health and social care services for older people. In order to lead this programme of change and reform we will appoint a National Director for Services for Older People this autumn.

15.22 We will improve standards across the range of services that older people use. Wherever older people are cared for, we will expect that both they and their carers will be treated in a way which respects their dignity, privacy and autonomy. This is not an addition to care provision, it is an integral part of good care.

16

The reform programme

Introduction

16.1 Expanding and reforming the NHS takes time. Change of this nature and on this scale does not happen overnight. This is not an excuse. It is a simple fact of life. It takes time to train and recruit the extra doctors, nurses and other staff the NHS needs, just as it takes time to build and equip modern NHS facilities. The resources are now in place. Delivery of the programme set out in this NHS Plan will provide the reforms the health service needs.

16.2 The process of modernisation is already underway. The internal market has gone and we have already started to build modern, responsive NHS services. The pace of improvement will now accelerate. Some improvements can be achieved quickly, others will take time.

16.3 The reform programme up to 2003/04 will be based on the settlement announced in the Budget on 21 March. We have been disciplined in determining how much progress we can make, and in the phasing of the proposals. This is an ambitious plan but a deliverable plan.

'Must do' targets

16.4 A key message arising from the consultation with the NHS in formulating this Plan was that it needs a small focused set of targets to drive change. Too many targets simply overwhelm the service.

16.5   This NHS Plan provides the clear, focused targets the Service has asked for. A small core of targets form the Department of Health's Public Service Agreement with the Treasury.

16.6   The targets are:

For the NHS

- reduce the maximum wait for an outpatient appointment to 3 months and the maximum wait for inpatient treatment to 6 months by the end of 2005

- patients will receive treatment at a time that suits them in accordance with their clinical need: two thirds of all outpatient appointments and inpatient elective admissions will be pre-booked by 2003/04 on the way to 100% pre-booking by 2005

- guaranteed access to a primary care professional within 24 hours and to a primary care doctor within 48 hours by 2004

- to secure year-on-year improvements in patient satisfaction including standards of cleanliness and food as measured by independently audited surveys

- reduce substantially the mortality rates from major killers by 2010; from heart disease by at least 40% in people under 75; from cancer by at least 20% in people under 75; and from suicide and undetermined injury by at least 20%. Key to the delivery of this target will be implementing the National Service Frameworks for Coronary Heart Disease, and Mental Health and the National Cancer Plan

- our objective is to narrow the health gap in childhood and throughout life between socio-economic groups and between the most deprived areas and the rest of the country. Specific national targets will be developed with stakeholders and experts early in 2001

- the cost of care commissioned from trusts which perform well against indicators of fair access, quality and responsiveness, will become the benchmark for the NHS. Everyone will be expected to reach the level of the best over the next five years, with agreed milestones for 2003/04.

For the NHS in partnership with social services

- provide high quality pre-admission and rehabilitation care to older people to help them live as independently as possible by reducing preventable hospitalisation and ensuring year-on-year reductions in delays in moving people over 75 on from hospital. We expect at least 130,000 people to benefit and we will monitor progress in the Performance Assessment Framework

- increase the participation of problem drug users in drug treatment programmes by 55% by 2004, and 100% by 2008.

For social services

Improve the life chances for children in care by:

- improving the level of education, training and employment outcomes for care leavers aged 19, so that levels for this group are at least 75% of those achieved by all young people in the same area by March 2004

- increasing the percentage of children in care who achieve at least five grade A* to C GCSEs to 15% by 2004

- giving them the care and guidance needed to narrow the gap by 2004 between the proportion of children in care and their peers who are cautioned or convicted

- maximising the contribution adoption can make to providing permanent families for children; a specific target will be set in the light of the Prime Minister's review of adoption services.

The next steps

16.7   Implementation of this NHS Plan begins immediately:

- during August 2000, new resources to increase the number of heart operations will be allocated to the NHS

- by September 2000, the Modernisation Board will be in place

- by autumn 2000, the new NHS Chief Executive will be appointed

- in the autumn, the Modernisation Board will agree and publish a detailed implementation programme for the NHS Plan

- in the autumn, we will for the first time provide health authorities with three year allocations, rather than annualised allocations allowing the NHS the financial stability needed at a time of service modernisation.

Conclusion

16.8   This NHS Plan is ambitious and radical. It is based on investment and reform. Investment to expand staff and services in the NHS. Reform to get the best value from this extra investment in the NHS. It represents a fundamental package of reforms to address the systemic weaknesses inherent in the NHS since its creation in 1948.

16.9   The NHS Plan has been developed with the help of leading doctors and nurses, therapists and other NHS staff, top NHS managers, patient and citizens' representatives. They have signed up to the principles on which it is based. The Government believes the Plan provides the basis for a national effort to reform the National Health Service.

16.10   Over the weeks and months ahead, the joint effort and service-wide co-operation, which marked the production of the NHS Plan, will be harnessed to deliver it. This scale of investment will be felt at every level of the NHS. Reform will require change at every level. Change will be led by key modernisers from within the service itself.

16.11   There is overwhelming support across the country and across the Service to see the NHS improved and reformed. Now, the necessary resources are in place. The reform programme is set out. It will take time to deliver but our vision of an NHS designed around the patient will become a reality.

Annex 1

The public's concerns about the NHS today

More, better paid staff

A1.1 People want more nurses, doctors, therapists and scientists in the NHS, to ease the pressure on services and allow patients to be seen more quickly. They want them doing less paperwork. People believe staff deserve better pay. Twenty-seven per cent of the public responding to the public consultation wanted more NHS staff and better pay for doctors and nurses.

Reduced waiting times

Staff: "The NHS culture of waiting has to end."

Community Nurse: "Patients get ill 24 hours a day. Develop access when they need it."

Staff: "Sometimes patients have to wait so long we have to let them go and then send their drugs after them by taxi."

A1.2 People think the NHS is too slow. Delay, cancellation and unreliability are commonplace in every part of the system. Seven out of ten people think waiting lists and waiting times for operations are too long. More than six in ten think patients have to wait too long to be seen in casualty. Trolley waits are regarded as unacceptable. Almost a third of patients would like to see GPs extend their opening hours in the evenings and about a quarter want them to open on Saturdays.

New ways of working

Public: "Cleanliness, cleanliness, cleanliness – employ more cleaners in hospital"

Staff: "Develop a modern matron – someone to get things done, someone patient focused."

A1.3   Patients want to see different ways of working in the NHS. The consultation with the public supported the return of 'Matron' – with authority on the ward, in charge of getting the basics right, without getting bogged down in bureaucracy.

A1.4   Members of the public told us they wanted to see a reduction in the amount of administration and bureaucracy in the service, with more resources to be invested in frontline services and better IT systems instead. Patients want to see all NHS staff used more effectively, with an expanded role for GPs and pharmacists.

Care centred on patients

Staff: "We must improve peoples' experience of the NHS. Often this means little things to improve dignity, comfort and convenience."

A1.5   People are concerned that too much of what the NHS does is dictated by the needs of the system rather than the needs of the patient. The NHS has a reputation for unreliable timekeeping so when people get an appointment they are sceptical about whether it will be cancelled. About half of people think cancellation rates for operations need to be improved. The inability of the NHS to work properly with social services is a real cause of concern for elderly patients.

Quality of care

A1.6   While people continue to show real faith in the integrity and professionalism of NHS staff, they see problems in some staff attitudes. Patients feel talked at too much and listened to not enough. More than 10% of people are dissatisfied with their experiences as inpatients. This rises to almost 20% in some parts of the country. People want to see better and more consistent services for treating cancer and heart disease. Forty per cent of people think cancer services need to be improved significantly.

Better facilities

A1.7   People want to see the basics put right. Half of people think the condition of hospital buildings needs to be improved. Few people are complimentary about hospital food. One survey found almost a third of patients needed help eating meals but did not always get it. Dirty hospitals are a big concern. Patients are concerned at mixed sex wards.

Better local services

A1.8 Members of the public said that they wanted to see better transport and access to services, better community care, and more joined up services. They also said that they wanted more community and cottage hospitals.

Better treatment for NHS staff

Staff: Clinical Nurse Specialist: "My difficulties rest with the limited clerical support given to me, resulting in my time being used to stand over a photocopier, check on clinic changes, order stationery etc."

Nurse: "We want to treat our patients better. We want to be treated better too."

A1.9 People trust, value and admire the dedication, expertise and compassion of staff who work day-in and day-out for patients. Ninety per cent of the public are satisfied with the way doctors do their jobs, 96% are satisfied with the way nurses do their jobs. They are the most trusted professions in the country. The public wants to see better rewards for staff for the hard work they put in on behalf of patients.

A national service

Member of the public interviewed by the Office for Public Management: "Keep the NHS, make it a truly national service with high quality treatment wherever you are – people want to be confident that the NHS will provide excellent treatment and care which is consistent across the country."

A1.10 There is major public concern about variations in services. There is a frustration that one part of the country can offer an excellent service, while a neighbouring area struggles to meet basic needs. People want the NHS to be a truly national service, providing high quality treatment wherever they live.

More prevention

Staff: "We still look after our cars better than we look after our health."

A1.11 There is an enormous public appetite for information on health. People want to be healthy, but do not see the NHS providing much support for doing so. Sixty five per cent of the public think the NHS should spend more time and money on maintaining people in good health by better provision of services and information.

Annex 2

Modernisation action team members

Bob Abberley, *Head of Health, Unison*

Professor Sir George Alberti, *President, Royal College of Physicians*

Professor Louis Appleby, *Professor of Psychiatry, University of Manchester*

Malcolm Bailey, *Murray Hall Community Health Trust*

Millie Banerjee, *Senior Vice President, ICONET Business Management*

David Behan, *Director of Social Services, Greenwich London Borough Council*

John Belcher, *Chief Executive, Anchor Housing Trust*

Professor Donald Berwick MD, *President of the Institute of Healthcare Improvement*

Professor Helen Bevan, *Director of Redesign, National Patients' Access Team Trust*

Professor Alison Blenkinsopp, *Department of Medicine Management, Keele University*

Dr Ian Bogle, *Chairman of Council, British Medical Association*

Dr Jonathan Boyce, *Audit Commission*

Dr Roger Boyle, *National Heart Director*

Alistair Bridges, *HM Treasury*

Mark Britnell, *Deputy Chief Executive, University Hospital, Birmingham*

Gill Brook, *Clinical Nurse Specialist, Diana Princess of Wales Children's Hospital, Birmingham*

Yve Buckland, *Chair, Health Development Agency*

Jackie Carnell, *Director, Community Practitioners and Health Visitors Association*

Ian Carruthers, *Chief Executive, Dorset Health Authority*

Karen Castille, *Programme Director – Emergency Services, National Patients' Access Team*

Harry Cayton, *Chief Executive, Alzheimers' Disease Society*

Dr John Chisholm, *Chairman, General Practitioners' Committee, British Medical Association*

Dr Rakesh Chopra, *Lintonville Medical Group*

Paddy Cooney, *Chief Executive, Somerset Partnership NHS and Social Care Trust*

Yvette Cooper MP, *Parliamentary Under-Secretary of State for Public Health*

Angela Coulter, *Chief Executive, Picker Institute Europe*

Professor Ara Darzi, *Professor of Surgery, St Mary's Hospital, London*

Karlene Davis, *General Secretary, Royal College of Midwives*

John Denham MP, *Minister of State for Health*

Professor Paul Dieppe, *Director, MRC National Collaboration on Health Services Research*

Professor Liam Donaldson, *Chief Medical Officer, Department of Health*

Heather Drabble, Director of Nursing, *Northern General Hospital NHS Trust*

Kay East, *Chair, College of Occupational Therapists*

Margaret Edwards, *Chief Executive, Heatherwood and Wexham Park Hospitals NHS Trust*

Mike Farrar, *Head of Primary Care, Department of Health*

John Flook, *Director of Finance, County Durham Health Authority*

Andrew Foster, *Chairman, Wigan and Leigh Health Services NHS Trust*

Andrew Foster, *Controller, Audit Commission*

Dr Debbie Freake, *Adelaide Medical Centre, Newcastle-upon-Tyne*

Bob Gann, *Director, The Help for Health Trust*

Lance Gardner, *Personal Medical Service Project, Salford*

Mark Goldman, *Medical Director, Birmingham Heartlands Hospital*

Dr Barbara Hakin, *Chair, South and West Bradford PCG*

Professor Aidan Halligan, *NHS Director of Clinical Governance*

Professor Chris Ham, *Department of Health*

Christine Hancock, *General Secretary, Royal College of Nursing*

Judy Hargadon, *Chief Executive, Barnet Health Authority*

Dr Peter Hawker, *Chairman CCSC, British Medical Association*

Dr Nicholas Hicks, *Department of Health*

David Highton, *Chief Executive, Oxford Radcliffe Hospitals NHS Trust*

Suzanne Hinchcliffe, *Nurse Executive Director, Barnsley District General Hospital NHS Trust*

Christopher Holcombe, *Consultant Breast Surgeon, Royal Liverpool and Broadgreen University Hospitals NHS Trust*

Peter Homa, *Director, Commission for Health Improvement*

William Hubbard, *Consultant Cardiologist and Clinical Director of Cardiology, Royal United Hospital, Bath*

Jan Hull, *Health Promotion Manager, Somerset Health Authority*

Lord Hunt of King's Health, *Parliamentary Under-Secretary of State*

Dr Ruth Hussey, *Director of Public Health, Liverpool Health Authority*

John Hutton MP, *Minister of State for Health*

Barry Jackson, *President, Royal College of Surgeons of England*

Dianne Jeffrey, *Chair, Community Healthcare Service, North Derbyshire NHS Trust*

Sue Jennings, *Head of the National Patients' Access Team*

James Johnson, *Chairman, Joint Consultants' Committee*

Mark Jones, *Primary Care Policy and Practice Advisor, Royal College of Nursing*

Dawn Killey, *Healthcare Assistant, The Eye Unit, Royal Bolton Hospital*

Gavin Larner, *Department of Health*

Rebecca Lawrence, *HM Treasury*

Dr Suzanna Lawrence OBE, *Chair, Leeds Health Authority*

Jo Lenaghan, *Department of Health*

Melinda Letts, *Chairwoman, Long-Term Medical Conditions Alliance*

Dr David Lloyd, *Ridgeway Surgery, North Harrow*

Neil Lockwood, *Chief Executive, Sandwell Health Authority*

Sir Alexander Macara, *Chairman, National Heart Forum*

Angela Machatuta, *Director of Professional Development, Bedfordshire and Luton Community Trust*

Professor Dame Jill Macleod-Clark, *Deputy Dean and Head of Nursing and Midwifery, University of Southampton*

Professor Sir Roderick MacSween, *Chairman, Academy of the Medical Royal Colleges*

Shaffi Mahate, *Birmingham Women's Healthcare NHS Trust*

Professor Sir Michael Marmot, *Professor of Epidemiology and Public Health, University College London*

Andrew Mawson OBE, *Co-Director, Community Action Network*

Jim McCaffery, *Director of Personnel and Development, Leeds Teaching Hospital*

Bill McCarthy, *Deputy Director of Finance and Performance, NHS Executive, Department of Health*

Professor Jim McEwen, *President, Faculty of Public Health, Royal College of Physicians*

Neil McKay, *Acting Chief Executive, NHS Executive, Department of Health*

Barbara Meredith, *Vice Chair, Patients' Forum*

Gopa Mitra MBE, *Proprietary Association of Great Britain*

Delyth Morgan, *Chief Executive, Breakthrough Breast Cancer*

Sarah Mullally, *Chief Nursing Officer, Department of Health*

Dr Derek Munday, *Chair, Wokingham PCG*

Richard Murray, *Department of Health*

Rabbi Julia Neuberger, *Chief Executive, The King's Fund*

Sally Newman, *Superintendent Physiotherapist, Withington Hospital*

Tony Newton OBE (Rt Hon Lord Newton of Braintree), *Chair, North East Essex Mental Health NHS Trust*

Mary Ney, *Director of Social Services, Harrow*

John Nicholson, *Chief Executive, UK Public Health Association*

Zoe Nicholson, *Assistant Director of Performance and Planning, East Sussex, Brighton and Hove Health Authority*

Dr John Oldham, *Head, National Primary Care Development Team*

Sue Page, *Chief Executive, Northumbria Healthcare NHS Trust*

David Panter, *Chief Executive, Hillingdon PCT*

Dr Chai Patel, *Chief Executive, Westminster Healthcare plc*

Denise Platt, *Chief Inspector of Social Services, Department of Health*

John Pope, *Chief Executive, North West London Hospitals NHS Trust*

Dr Anton Pozniak, *Consultant in GU and HIV, Chelsea and Westminster Healthcare NHS Trust*

Professor Mike Pringle, *Chairman of Council, Royal College of General Practitioners*

John Ransford, *Head of Social Affairs, Health and Housing, Local Government Association*

Professor Sir Michael Rawlins, *Chair of National Institute for Clinical Excellence*

Eoin Redahan, *Director of Public Relations, Stroke Association*

John Renshaw, *Chairman, Executive Board, British Dental Association*

Professor Mike Richards, *National Cancer Director and Sainsbury Professor of Palliative Medicine, St Thomas' Hospital*

Marianne Rigge, *Director, College of Health*

Nick Ross, *Broadcaster*

John Rostill, *Chief Executive, Walsall Hospitals NHS Trust*

Liz Sargeant, *General Manager of Rehabilitation Services, Hinchingbrooke Healthcare NHS Trust*

Janet Saunders, *Ward Sister, Acute care of the Elderly, Bath and West Community NHS Trust*

Dr Jenny Simpson, *Chief Executive, British Association of Medical Managers*

Gulab Singh MBE, *Deputy Health Promotion Manager, North West Lancashire Health Authority*

Pam Smith, *Medical Laboratories Scientific Officer, Winchester and Eastleigh Healthcare NHS Trust*

Professor Peter C Smith, *Centre for Health Economics, University of York*

Simon Stevens, *Department of Health*

Lesley Stirling-Baxter, *Chief Officer, Bradford CHC*

Paul Streets, *Chief Executive, British Diabetic Association*

Councillor Rita Stringfellow, *Chair of Housing, Health and Social Affairs Committee, Local Government Association*

Gisela Stuart MP, *Parliamentary Under-Secretary of State for Health*

Hazel Stuteley, *Community Nurse Health Advisor, Cornwall Healthcare Trust*

Hugh Taylor, *Director of Human Resources, NHS Executive, Department of Health*

Steven Thornton, *Chief Executive, NHS Confederation*

John Van Reenen, *Department of Health*

David Walden, *Head of Social Care Policy, Department of Health*

Moira Wallace, *Social Exclusion Unit, Cabinet Office*

Edmund Waterhouse, *Department of Health*

Sir William Wells, *Regional Chair, NHS Executive South East Regional Office*

Sue West, Dietician, *Pindersfields and Pontefract Hospitals NHS Trust*

Wendy Wheeler, *Health Visitor, City and Hackney Community Services NHS Trust*

Diana Whitworth, *Chief Executive, Carers National Association*

Jo Williams, *President, Association of Directors of Social Services*

Sir Nicholas Young, *Chief Executive, Macmillan Cancer Relief*

Dr Paul Zollinger-Read, *Primary Care Lead, National Patients' Access Team*

Annex 3

Department of Health Public Service Agreement

Aim

A3.1 To transform the health and social care system so that it produces faster, fairer services that deliver better health and tackles health inequalities.

Objectives and performance targets

Objective I: improving health outcomes for everyone

A3.2 Reduce substantially the mortality rates from major killers by 2010: from heart disease by at least 40% in people under 75; from cancer by at least 20% in people under 75; and from suicide and undetermined injury by at least 20%. Key to the delivery of this target will be implementing the National Service Frameworks for coronary heart disease and mental health and the National Cancer Plan.

A3.3 Our objective is to narrow the health gap in childhood and throughout life between socio-economic groups and between the most deprived areas and the rest of the country. Specific national targets will be developed in consultation with external stakeholders and experts early in 2001.

Objective II: improving patient and carer experience of the NHS and social services

A3.4 Patients will receive treatment at a time that suits them in accordance with their clinical need: two thirds of all outpatient appointments and inpatient elective admissions will be pre-booked by 2003/04 on the way to 100% pre-booking by 2005.

A3.5 Reduce the maximum wait for an outpatient appointment to 3 months and the maximum wait for inpatient treatment to 6 months by the end of 2005.

A3.6 To secure year-on-year improvements in patient satisfaction, including standards of cleanliness and food, as measured by independently audited local surveys.

Objective III: effective delivery of appropriate care

A3.7 Provide high quality pre-admission and rehabilitation care to older people to help them live as independently as possible by reducing preventable hospitalisation and ensuring year-on-year reductions in delays in moving people over 75 on from hospital. We expect at least 130,000 people to benefit and we shall monitor progress in the Performance Assessment Framework.

A3.8 Improve the life chances for children in care by:

- improving the level of education, training and employment outcomes for care leavers aged 19, so that levels for this group are at least 75% of those achieved by all young people in the same area by March 2004

- improving the educational attainment of children and young people in care by increasing from 6% in 1998 to 15% in 2004 the proportion of children leaving care aged 16 and over with 5 GCSEs at grade A*–C.

- giving them the care and guidance needed to narrow the gap by 2004 between the proportion of children in care who are cautioned

- maximising the contribution adoption can make to providing permanent families for children; a specific target will be set in the light of the Prime Minister's review of adoption services.

A3.9 Increase the participation of problem drug users in drug treatment programmes by 55% by 2004 and by 100% by 2008.

Objective IV: fair access

A3.10 Guaranteed access to a primary care professional within 24 hours and to a primary care doctor within 48 hours by 2004.

Objective V: value for money

A3.11 The cost of care commissioned from trusts which perform well against indicators of fair access, quality and responsiveness, will become the benchmark for the NHS. Everyone will be expected to reach the level of the best over the next 5 years, with agreed milestones for 2003/04.

Statement of accountability

A3.11 The Secretary of State for Health is accountable for the delivery of the targets set out in this Public Service Agreement.

Printed in the UK for The Stationery Office Limited
On behalf of the Controller of Her Majesty's Stationery Office
Dd 5069371   7/00   019585   TJ 002203